ANOVA
Repeated Measures

ELLEN R. GIRDEN
Nova University

SAGE PUBLICATIONS
The International Professional Publishers
Newbury Park   London   New Delhi

For information address:

 SAGE Publications, Inc.
2455 Teller Road
Newbury Park, California 91320

SAGE Publications Ltd.
6 Bonhill Street
London EC2A 4PU
United Kingdom

SAGE Publications India Pvt. Ltd.
M-32 Market
Greater Kailash I
New Delhi 110 048 India

Printed in the United States of America

Girden, Ellen R.
    ANOVA: repeated measures / Ellen R. Girden.
        p.   cm.—(Sage university papers series. Quantitative
applications in the social sciences; 84)
      Includes bibliographical references (p.   ).
      ISBN 0-8039-4257-5 (pb)
      1. Social sciences—Statistical methods.   2. Analysis of variance.
    I. Title.   II. Series.
    HA29.G567   1992
    300′.1′519538—dc20   91-34563

93 94 95 96 10 9 8 7 6 5 4 3 2

Sage Production Editor: Astrid Virding

When citing a university paper, please use the proper form. Remember to cite the current Sage University Paper series title and include the paper number. One of the following formats can be adapted (depending on the style manual used):

(1) GIRDEN, E. R. (1992) ANOVA: Repeated Measures. Sage University Paper Series on Quantitative Applications in the Social Sciences, 07-084. Newbury Park, CA: Sage.

OR

(2) Girden, E. R. (1992) *ANOVA: Repeated Measures* (Sage University Paper series on Quantitative Applications in the Social Sciences, series no. 07-084). Newbury Park, CA: Sage.

CONTENTS

SERIES EDITOR'S INTRODUCTION

In traditional analysis of variance (ANOVA), first individuals may be assigned randomly to different treatment groups, then effects assessed. Classic ANOVA procedures formed the basis of the first monograph in our series (Iversen & Norpoth, 1976). Although this design offers a well-established paradigm for experimental research, of late the repeated measures approach to ANOVA has emerged as a lively alternative.

Unlike a classic design, a group of individuals may be subjected to more than one treatment. This approach has certain obvious advantages. The number of individuals needed for the design is much smaller. Further, the group serves as its own control. Take as an example a political science experimenter who wants to measure affective response to the pictures of six different presidential candidates. In a traditional approach, that experiment might require six treatment groups with 30 subjects each, for a total of 180 subjects. As an alternative, a repeated measures approach might use only 30 subjects, simply administering each of the six treatments to those in that same group.

Of course, there are disadvantages to a repeated measures strategy. Serious attrition of subjects over multiple treatments can occur. Also, the order of treatment administration can bias the results because of practice, carry-over, or fatigue. In this monograph, Dr. Girden gives tools for countering these disadvantages. The attrition problem, for example, might be dealt with after careful consideration of different ways of handling missing data. The order effects generally can be overcome by counterbalancing. Beyond these design problems, there are analysis difficulties as well. In particular, the usual F test is almost certainly biased, requiring a sphericity correction. Girden gives a full discussion of the sphericity problem and its implications for significance testing, a topic often neglected in the published research applications of repeated measures.

This monograph offers more thorough coverage than is available in general texts, moving from single-factor studies to two-factor studies (with repeated measures on one or both factors) to three-factor studies.

Additive and nonadditive models are included, the partitioning of sums of squares is given in detail, tests are offered for when the general sphericity condition fails to hold, and estimation of strength of association is discussed (including difficulties with the widely used omega squared). In her explication, Girden draws on examples from education, psychology, medicine, and sociology. For these areas, as well as the experimental branches of other social sciences, analysis of variance with repeated measures holds much promise. This monograph will be useful to any scholar wanting to apply this relatively new and sometimes controversial technique to her or his work.

—*Michael S. Lewis-Beck*
Series Editor

ANOVA
Repeated Measures

ELLEN R. GIRDEN
Nova University

1. INTRODUCTION

Analysis of variance, in its simplest form, is a general procedure for isolating the sources of variability in a set of measurements. The purpose is to determine the extent to which the effect of an independent variable is a major component. Techniques for analyzing data from independent groups of individuals have been presented elsewhere (cf. Iversen & Norpoth, 1976). This monograph focuses on situations involving the repeated measurement of the same group of individuals. When separate groups of individuals are studied, the number of individuals required is some multiple of the combined levels (called *treatment levels*) of each factor that is introduced. For example, an investigation of the effect of three different drugs (each a level) at two different dosages (two levels) would require six different groups of individuals. Supposing a minimum of 10 individuals per group, a total of 60 individuals would have to be recruited. When the same individuals can take part in all conditions of the study, fewer participants are required. For example, that same study might employ only 10 individuals, each measured six times.

When separate groups of individuals are tested, a major concern is that each initially is equivalent with respect to the dependent variable, so that posttest differences can be attributed to the specific variables that were introduced. Equivalency can be facilitated by the random assignment of individuals to the various groups or by matching groups on the basis of some relevant pretest. Despite these drawbacks (large numbers and the need for equivalency), separate groups are mandated when the independent variable includes characteristics of participants (e.g., different IQs, levels of anxiety, gender, etc.), different treatments (e.g., therapy), different instructions, or any type of variation such that serving in one condition would have a dramatic

1

effect on serving in another. In other research situations, the investigator may *have to* test the same group of individuals (e.g., longitudinal studies, learning studies involving trials) or may *have a choice* between measuring the same individuals or measuring separate groups. These situations now are considered.

2. REPEATED MEASURES SITUATIONS

Suppose that you want to know whether individuals would work harder to buy food if its cost increased. Intuitively the answer is yes; everyone has to eat. One way to vary the amount of work is to increase the number of responses an individual has to make before he or she gains access to food. The food is harder to get; indirectly its cost has increased. Although humans could participate in the study, pigeons are easier to train. In order to gain 10 seconds of access to food, the pigeons would have to make 5, 10, 15, or 20 responses, named A, B, C, and D. Each set of responses is called a *fixed ratio*. For example, A represents a ratio of 5:1—five responses for one 10-second access to food. In this situation it would be inappropriate to use separate groups of pigeons randomly assigned to each fixed ratio. Your interest is in whether the number of responses per unit of time *progressively* increases from representations of A to B to C to D. If a situation calls for relative or comparative behaviors or judgments of any kind, the use of independent groups would be inappropriate.

In other situations the intent may be to compare the relative effectiveness of different drugs, or dosages of the same drug, when few individuals are available. Rather than randomly assigning them to the various conditions, the same individuals can be measured at all levels. The advantage of such a study is that differences in posttreatment measures cannot be attributed to individual characteristics (e.g., motivation, intelligence). In other words, equivalency before treatment is not a problem, because each individual serves as his or her own control. In either case, the design of the investigation is termed *repeated measures,* because the same individuals are measured on a number of occasions corresponding to each treatment level. It also is referred to as a *randomized block* design, with each individual designated as a "block."

Advantages and Disadvantages

The advantages of testing the same individuals throughout a study are that fewer subjects are required and equivalent pretreatment measures are not a matter of concern. A major disadvantage is the risk of attrition if participants require multiple tests. The other technical disadvantage is that the order in which levels are administered must be controlled to minimize the effects of practice, fatigue, and carry-over. With only one order, an improvement in performance may be attributed to treatment or practice. A decline may be attributed to treatment or fatigue. Inconsistent changes in performance may be attributed to treatment or to a carry-over effect of the residuals of prior treatment. There also may be a *latency effect,* an effect of treatment that is not evident until a second treatment is introduced. Most often these order effects can be controlled by counterbalancing. Carry-over can be minimized by lengthening the time between treatments; latency, however, is harder to control.

Counterbalancing

Counterbalancing is a way of presenting the different levels of treatment, such that each one (a) occurs equally often at each stage of practice (i.e., each is the first to be presented, the second to be presented, etc.) and (b) precedes as many times as it follows each level. The intent is to counteract fatigue, practice, and carry-over effects. With an even number of levels and a number of individuals that is some multiple of it, these two requirements can be met by applying the following guideline:

$$1, 2, n, 3, n - 1, 4, n - 2, \text{etc.}$$

Each number refers to a treatment level. If four levels are to be tested, then the guideline reduces to 1, 2, 4, 3, the first order of the levels. Each subsequent order is derived by adding "1" to the numbers of the preceding order. The second order would be 2 (1 + 1), 3 (2 + 1), 1 (4 + 1 does not apply), 4 (3 + 1). If the levels correspond to presenting A(1), B(2), C(3), and D(4), then a suitable sequence of orders, following the guideline, is found in Table 2.1. Each fixed ratio occurs once at each stage of practice, and each ratio precedes and follows

TABLE 2.1

Orders of Presenting Four Fixed Ratios

Pigeon	First	Stages of Practice		
		Second	Third	Fourth
1	A	B	D	C
2	B	C	A	D
3	C	D	B	A
4	D	A	C	B

every other ratio the same number of times. For example, A precedes B once (for the first pigeon) and follows B once (for the third pigeon). A precedes C once (for the fourth pigeon) and follows C once (for the second pigeon). Finally, A precedes D once (for the second pigeon) and follows D once (for the fourth pigeon). When responses under all ratios representing A, B, C, and D are gathered together, mean differences should not be due to practice, fatigue, or carry-over. With an odd number of levels, the requirements can be fulfilled by first using the procedure just described to derive one set of orders and then constructing another set by reversing the top row (i.e., 3, 4, 2, 1) and repeating the procedure.

Application of Repeated Measures Designs

Repeated measures studies have been conducted in virtually all behavioral and social sciences: psychology, medicine, education, sociology, political science, economics, business, and industry. Here are some examples of representative studies. Some have introduced a single independent variable to one group of individuals, others include more than one group and/or more than one variable, with repeated measures made on at least one of them.

1. Educators find that the quality of students' writing is mediocre when geared for teacher evaluation, even though a more skillful level could be achieved if students had to write for a different audience, as demonstrated by Cohen and Riel (1989). One class of seventh graders wrote an essay for their semester grade and a week later wrote on the same topic for peers in another country. Another class had the same assignments in the opposite order. Data were analyzed by simple ANOVA for repeated measures.

2. Business suffers when work is not intrinsically rewarding and challenging. Therefore researchers have sought factors that can increase intrinsic motivation. Hirst (1988) considered job complexity and goal setting. One group of adults worked toward a reasonable goal and another worked toward a difficult, unreasonable goal. Half of each group started with a simple task, followed by a more difficult, challenging one. The other half had the reverse procedure. Data were analyzed by a two-way ANOVA with repeated measures on one factor (intrinsic motivation).

3. Little data exist on the appropriate use of restraint and/or seclusion in managing unruly behavior of psychiatric patients, and there is little agreement among professionals and lawyers regarding what constitutes (and is perceived as) the least restraining techniques. In order to provide some data, realistic situations requiring varying amounts of restraints were presented to experienced and inexperienced psychiatric patients and staff members of a maximum security institution. Comparisons were made on which technique each group considered to be the most effective for each situation (repeated measures) and the psychological effect each might have on the patient (Harris, Rice, & Preston, 1989).

4. Secondary school students should be better able to apply what they have learned if they are instructed in application rather than rote memorization. Students with learning disabilities were given 12 consecutive days of training on improving health factors that would increase longevity. For the first part of each day, all students had structured lessons. For the second part of the day, half of the students continued with structured review of the material and conventional application techniques (e.g., keeping track of their diet). The other half worked with computer simulation exercises in analyzing health problems and changing them to alleviate the problems. All students were tested for retention 1 day after the lessons and again 2 weeks later. Data were analyzed by a two-way ANOVA with repeated measures on one factor (Woodward, Carnine, & Gersten, 1988).

5. When handicapped and nonhandicapped children attend the same school, peer interactions are difficult. Two programs to facilitate greater integration were compared. Nonhandicapped fourth-, fifth-, and sixth-graders were paired with handicapped peers and attended peer tutoring or special-friends interaction sessions. Interactions between pairs were rated and compared across the 8-week period (Cole, Vandercook, & Rynders, 1988).

6. The extent to which students (future decision makers) remain committed to their decisions may depend on the realism of the situation,

job insecurity, resistance to changing their policy, and anxiety level. Students with high and low trait anxiety were randomly assigned to high and low job-insecurity conditions, crossed with high and low policy-resistance conditions, during three phases of a study and were measured for the extent to which they remained committed to decisions regarding raising revenues for the university while acting as director of special funding. Realism, the extent to which they felt threatened during each phase, was determined by measuring state anxiety at the end of each phase. Levels of state anxiety (repeated measures) were analyzed as a function of trait anxiety, job insecurity, policy resistance, and the three phases of the study (Moore, Jensen, & Hauck, 1990).

With this background, the designs and analyses of repeated measures studies follow. Examples of studies from other disciplines appear in each chapter.

3. SINGLE-FACTOR STUDIES

We begin with the simplest situation: All individuals are exposed to each level of a single independent variable (factor). The following study is a modification of one conducted by O'Connell (1988). Assume that four pigeons have been trained to step on a treadle 5, 10, 15, and 20 times in order to produce a light that signals 10 seconds of access to food. Only one fixed ratio operates on any given day. Moreover, the pigeons peck at the light when it appears, although not required to do so (a phenomenon known as *autoshaping*). The rate of light-pecking constitutes the measure of amount of work (dependent variable). The number of pecks per minute, averaged over 4 days, is found in Table 3.1. The study was conducted to determine whether the pigeons will work harder as the cost of food increases. If they do not, then the four mean response rates should be about the same. If they do, then the response rates should be progressively higher. Indeed the four means are progressively larger. Our task is to determine whether these observed differences reasonably can be attributed to chance, or whether they reflect a likely "willingness" to work harder as the unit cost of food increases. Statistically, the null hypothesis (H_0: $\mu_A = \mu_B = \mu_C = \mu_D$) is being tested against the alternative (H_1: not all μs are equal).

TABLE 3.1
Rate of Responding Under Four Fixed Ratios by Four Subjects

Subject	A	B	C	D	Sum	Mean ($\bar{Y}_i$)
1	10	19	27	28	84	21.0
2	9	13	25	29	76	19.0
3	4	10	20	18	52	13.0
4	5	6	12	17	40	10.0
ΣY =	28	48	84	92	252	—
ΣY^2 =	222	666	1,898	2,238	5,024	—
$\bar{Y}_j$ =	7.0	12.0	21.0	23.0	—	15.75

The key to the solution lies in answering why any particular score (e.g., 19) differs from the overall grand mean of 15.75. There are two general responses. One assumes an additive, and the other an interactive, statistical guideline or model. The differences in models are of no practical consequence for the single-factor study, but they are relevant for more complex situations. Therefore they merit consideration.

Additive Model

One response to why a score (of 19) differs from the grand mean (of 15.75) is that the score results from the summative effect of a particular fixed ratio (B), organism (the first pigeon), and random error or unexplained factors affecting the organism at that time. If these four pigeons are considered to be a random sample from the population of pigeons that responded with ratios A, B, C, and D, then the population representations, parameters, of the three components of the difference between a score and the grand mean are reflected in the following guideline for the analysis:

$$Y_{ij} - \mu = \alpha_j + \pi_i + \varepsilon_{ij}.$$

Here Y_{ij} is the score of the ith pigeon (the first, etc.) in the jth column (fixed ratio A, B, C, D); μ is the population grand mean of response rates under all fixed ratios; α_j is the constant, fixed effect on rate of responding of the jth ratio ($\mu_j - \mu$); π_i is the effect of the ith pigeon on response rate $(\mu_i - \mu)$; and ε_{ij} is the random error of the ith pigeon under the jth fixed ratio $(Y_{ij} - \mu_i)$.

Given the stipulation that $\Sigma\alpha_j = 0$, the organism effects (π_i) are assumed to be independent of each other and to be normally distributed, with a mean equal to 0 and variance equal to σ_π^2 [N(0, σ_π^2)]. Likewise, random, experimental errors (ε_{ij}) are assumed to be independent of the organism effects and of each other and to be normally distributed, with a mean equal to 0 and variance equal to σ_ε^2 [N(0, σ_ε^2)]. This model assumes that the effect of each treatment level is constant for each organism; hence the effects simply add to organism effects. For this reason, the model is called an *additive* model. Although it is more powerful than a nonadditive model (a test for additivity is reported in Kirk, 1982), as we'll see later, a more common assumption is that treatment effects are not constant as organisms are exposed to the various levels. Thus we arrive at the alternate reason why a particular score differs from that of the grand mean.

Nonadditive Model

This approach proposes that a score differs from the grand mean for the reasons cited above, with the addition that the effect of the particular pigeon interacted with that of the particular fixed ratio, yielding the alternate statistical guideline:

$$Y_{ij} - \mu = \alpha_j + \pi_i + \pi\alpha_{ij} + \varepsilon_{ij}.$$

The only new term is $\pi\alpha_{ij}$, the pigeon by fixed ratio interaction $(Y_{ij} - \mu_i - \mu_j + \mu)$: variability that remains after the unique effect of the pigeon and fixed ratio have been removed. In actual practice, as we'll see, $\pi\alpha_{ij}$ and ε_{ij} cannot be calculated separately.

As in the additive model, $\Sigma\alpha_j = 0$, π_i, and ε_{ij} are independent, normally distributed, with means equal to 0. The respective distribution variances are σ_π^2 and σ_ε^2. The random variable $\pi\alpha_{ij}$ of each organism is independent of each of the others, but not of different treatment levels of the *same* organism. These are assumed to sum to 0 for the same organism, and to be normally distributed, with a mean equal to 0 and variance equal to $[(J - 1)/J]\sigma_{\pi\alpha}^2$. The lack of independence among interaction variables and observations on the same organisms leads to certain validity assumptions underlying the repeated measures analysis, to be addressed later.

The analysis of sources of variability between scores and the grand mean proceeds with estimations of each component. Hence, the grand mean is estimated by $\overline{Y}_g$, the mean of all 16 scores. The effect of each fixed ratio, α_j, is estimated by the difference between each fixed-ratio mean and the grand mean, $\overline{Y}_j - \overline{Y}_g$. The effect of each pigeon, π_i, is estimated by the difference between each pigeon's mean and the grand mean, $\overline{Y}_i - \overline{Y}_g$. This component, *between-subjects*, reflects differences among the subjects. The interaction component, $\pi\alpha_{ij}$, is estimated by $Y_{ij} - \overline{Y}_i - \overline{Y}_j + \overline{Y}_g$. Random error, ε_{ij}, would be estimated by $Y_{ij} - \overline{Y}_i$, the difference between a score and the pigeon's mean. This component, *within-subjects*, reflects variability within each subject's performance. Now, if all four components are determined for any individual, they yield a value larger than $Y_{ij} - \overline{Y}_g$, due to overlapping information. The between-subjects component provides unique information; the within-subjects component does not. A subject's score differs from its mean (within-subjects) because it is of a particular fixed ratio ($\overline{Y}_j - \overline{Y}_g$) and because the effect of that pigeon, along with random error, may have interacted with that of the particular fixed ratio. However, only one calculated value represents these two components. This is why $\alpha\pi_{ij}$ and ε_{ij} cannot be separated, although random error contributes to performance at each fixed ratio. Symbolically,

$$(Y_{ij} - \overline{Y}_g) \quad = \text{ between-subjects } + \text{ within-subjects}$$

$$(Y_{ij} - \overline{Y}_g) \quad = (\overline{Y}_i - \overline{Y}_g) \quad + (Y_{ij} - \overline{Y}_i)$$

$$\qquad\qquad = (\overline{Y}_i - \overline{Y}_g) \quad + [(\overline{Y}_j - \overline{Y}_g) + (Y_{ij} - \overline{Y}_i - \overline{Y}_j + \overline{Y}_g)].$$

These equalities are demonstrated with a score of 19 (see Table 3.1).

$$(Y_{ij} - \overline{Y}_g) \quad = (\overline{Y}_i - \overline{Y}_g) \quad + (Y_{ij} - \overline{Y}_i)$$

$$(19 - 15.75) = (21 - 15.75) \quad + (19 - 21)$$

$$3.25 \quad = 5.25 \quad + (-2)$$

$$\qquad\qquad = (\overline{Y}_i - \overline{Y}_g) \quad + [(\overline{Y}_j - \overline{Y}_g) + (Y_{ij} - \overline{Y}_i - \overline{Y}_j + \overline{Y}_g)]$$

$$= 5.25 \qquad + [(12 - 15.75) + (19 - 21 - 12 + 15.75)]$$

$$3.25 \qquad = 5.25 \qquad + [-3.75 + 1.75]$$

Clearly, the overall deviation of 3.25 points equals the between-subjects component of 5.25 plus the within-subjects component of -2. Further, the within-subjects component of -2 does equal the fixed-ratio effect of -3.75 plus the interaction effect of 1.75. If this analysis is performed on all 16 scores and all differences are squared and summed, we arrive at a working model to determine whether the rates of responding under the four fixed ratios differ or are statistically alike. The model is

$$SS_T = SS_S + SS_A + SS_{S \times A}.$$

Here, SS_T is the total sum of squared deviations of all scores from the grand mean, SS_S is the sum of squared deviations of subject means from the grand mean, SS_A is the sum of squared deviations of fixed-ratio means from the grand mean, and $SS_{S \times A}$ is the sum of squared deviations representing interaction.

The Analysis

The answer to whether pigeons will work harder as the price of food increases will be determined by the extent to which the fixed-ratio component of total variability (SS_A) exceeds that due to the remaining components. The 16 scores are in Table 3.1, with mean performances of the pigeons and means of the treatment levels.

$$SS_T = \sum (Y_{ij} - \overline{Y}_g)^2 = \sum [(10 - 15.75)^2 + \ldots + (17 - 15.75)^2] = \textit{1055}$$

The first component of SS_T is between-subjects variability. By definition this is the squared difference between each subject's mean and the grand mean, $(\overline{Y}_i - \overline{Y}_g)^2$, a component that will be identical at each fixed ratio. Because there are four different ratios, and therefore four scores per subject,

$$SS_S = J \sum [(\overline{Y}_i - \overline{Y}_g)^2] = 4[(21 - 15.75)^2 + \ldots + (10 - 15.75)^2] = \textit{315}.$$

TABLE 3.2
Summary of ANOVA for Repeated Measures on a Single Factor

Source	SS	df	MS	F
Subjects (S)	315	$n_j - 1 = 3$	105	—
Intervals (A)	683	$J - 1 = 3$	227.67	35.967
Residual	57	$(n_j - 1)(J - 1) = 9$	6.33	—
Total	1,055	15		

Similarly, by definition the fixed-ratio sum of squared deviations is the squared difference between fixed-ratio means and the grand mean, $(\overline{Y}_j - \overline{Y}_g)^2$. This operation also will result in an identical value for every subject under each treatment level. Because there are four pigeons at each treatment level,

$$SS_A = n_j \sum [(\overline{Y}_j - \overline{Y}_g)^2] = 4[(7 - 15.75)^2 + \ldots + (23 - 15.75)^2] = \quad 683.$$

The final component of SS_T is interaction. It is variability remaining, with the pigeon and fixed-ratio effects removed ($Y_{ij} - \overline{Y}_i - \overline{Y}_j + \overline{Y}_g$). This would be calculated for all 16 scores, or, given $SS_T = SS_S + SS_A + SS_{S \times A}$, the easier procedure is by subtraction:

$$SS_{S \times A} = SS_T - SS_S - SS_A = 1055 - 315 - 683 = \quad 57.$$

Because $SS_{S \times A}$ is variability after the other components have been removed from SS_T, it is also known as *residual* SS (SS_{res}).

The sums of squared deviations are in Table 3.2 with dfs and the final F ratio. The df for SS_{res} is the product of df for subjects ($S - 1$) and treatment ($J - 1$). The rationale for the F ratio (MS_A/MS_{res}) depends on the average values of the mean squares expected in the long run if a large number of MSs were determined: the expected mean square, E(MS).

The MS_S was calculated—an estimated variance reflecting variability in overall performance among subjects. This variability, in the long run, will have two sources of variance: that due to the uniqueness of the individual and that due to random error. Therefore, $E(MS_S) = J\sigma_\pi^2 + \sigma_\varepsilon^2$. MS_A, due to fixed-ratio effects, is derived from the scores of a random sample of four pigeons. Consequently, as is true of any mixed-effects statistical model (subjects are the random-effects variable and treatment is the constant, fixed-effects variable), the sum of interactions between the fixed-ratio and subject effects is not expected to equal zero in any given study (although it would if the entire population could be tested) and cannot be ruled out as a factor contributing to $E(MS_A)$ (cf. Iversen & Norpoth, 1976). Also, if the fixed ratio does affect rate of responding, variance due to this constant effect also contributes to $E(MS_A)$, as does random error. Thus $E(MS_A) = n_j \Sigma \alpha_j^2 / (J - 1) + \sigma_{\pi\alpha}^2 + \sigma_\varepsilon^2$. Finally, for the nonadditive model, the long-range expected value for residual, $E(MS_{res}) = \sigma_{\pi\alpha}^2 + \sigma_\varepsilon^2$, is a reflection of subject-treatment interaction effects not evident in the additive model and random error. Thus

$$
\begin{aligned}
E(MS_S) &= J\sigma_\pi^2 + \sigma_\varepsilon^2 \\
E(MS_A) &= n_j \sum \alpha_j^2 / (J - 1) + \sigma_{\pi\alpha}^2 + \sigma_\varepsilon^2 \\
E(MS_{res}) &= \qquad\qquad\qquad \sigma_{\pi\alpha}^2 + \sigma_\varepsilon^2
\end{aligned}
$$

As in any analysis of variance, the magnitude of an effect of an independent variable can be determined by forming an F ratio. The denominator contains an estimation of random error. The numerator contains an additional component to reflect systematic variability due to the independent variable. If $E(MS)$s are used to establish the appropriate ratio, the magnitude of the treatment effect is represented by the following:

$$
\frac{E(MS_A)}{E(MS_{res})} = \frac{n_j \sum \alpha_j / (J - 1) + \sigma_{\pi\alpha}^2 + \sigma_\varepsilon^2}{\sigma_{\pi\alpha}^2 + \sigma_\varepsilon^2}
$$

The only difference between numerator and denominator is the treatment component. All F ratios are formed along these lines, with one difference between the numerator and denominator:

$$
F = \frac{\text{hypothesized treatment effect + random error}}{\text{random error}}
$$

Therefore, if there is no treatment effect, the ratio would equal approximately 1.00. To the extent that there is a treatment effect, the ratio will exceed 1.00 (the numerator would be larger than the denominator).

On this basis, there is no error term appropriate to test the effect of the subjects (nor is this of interest). But the appropriate term for the fixed-ratio effect is MS_{res}. The ratio MS_A/MS_{res} will yield approximately 1.00 if all fixed ratios have the same effect, and a value greater than 1.00 if there is a differential effect of size of the fixed ratios on rate of responding. The obtained F ratio of 35.967, with df = 3, 9, is significant with $p < .01$ and indicates that pigeons will respond more rapidly as the cost of their food increases. The mean rates of responding corresponding to A, B, C, and D do differ, but exact mean differences cannot be discerned from the omnibus F ratio.

Had the study (inappropriately here) involved independent groups, the error term, MS_{within}, would have been 31 versus 6.33 and the F ratio would have been 7.34 versus 35.967. Here we see the biggest advantage of a repeated measures study: It provides a more powerful test of the null hypothesis because there are more sources of variability that can be extracted from error. However, this extraction is accompanied by a reduction in denominator df, here from 12 to 9, which tends to decrease power.

With the nonadditive model, the $E(MS_A)$ was seen to be a function of the constant effect of treatment, interaction, and random error. The additive model assumes no interaction, so that $E(MS_A) = n_j \Sigma \alpha^2/(J - 1) + \sigma_\varepsilon^2$. Similarly, with the interaction model, the $E(MS_S)$ was seen to be a function of the subject effect and random error. This is true of the additive model as well. Finally, with the interaction model, $E(MS_{res})$ was seen to be a function of interaction and random error. However, with the additive model, residual MS only is a function of random error: $E(MS_{res}) = \sigma_\varepsilon^2$. Because of this difference, it would be appropriate to test for the effect of the subjects (i.e., $[J\sigma_\pi^2 + \sigma_\varepsilon^2]/\sigma_\varepsilon^2$). More important, because MS_{res} in the long run only reflects error variance, the expected (additive model) residual variance is smaller and provides a more powerful test for treatment effects (i.e., $\sigma_\varepsilon^2 < \sigma_{\pi\alpha}^2 + \sigma_\varepsilon^2$). However, validity of the analysis depends on more than the appropriateness of the underlying model.

Validity Assumptions of Repeated Measures ANOVA

The validity of the repeated measures ANOVA rests on several assumptions that were recognized by R. A. Fisher in the 1940s but were not demonstrated until the 1950s (Box, 1954), with the result that many of the earlier studies involving repeated measures may have reached erroneous conclusions regarding the effect(s) of the independent variable(s). This is rather surprising when you consider that carry-over effects, not to mention practice and fatigue, were known well before the 1950s and resulted in the introduction of counterbalancing procedures to minimize them. Nonetheless, the earlier assumption, demonstrated by Box, was identified with compound symmetry. The later assumption, introduced by Huynh and Feldt (1970) and by Rouanet and Lépine (1970), is known as *circularity* or *sphericity.*

Compound Symmetry. Certain assumptions should be met in comparing an F ratio to a distribution with $(J - 1)$ and $(J - 1)(n_j - 1)$ degrees of freedom to establish whether MS_A/MS_{res} significantly deviates from a theoretical value. Variances within treatment levels are assumed to be homogeneous; observations among individuals are assumed to be independent and, because they are based on multiple dependent variables, to have a multivariate normal distribution. But observations made on the same individuals are correlated. The more highly correlated they are, the lower the MS_{res} (along with lower MS_A, but higher MS_S) and the more likely F will be significant.

A tacit, untested (until Box, 1954) assumption was that the degree of *covariation* between all pairs of treatment scores must be the same. This implies an equal effect of participating in one treatment level after another. Given that covariance, S_{ij}, equals $\Sigma(X - \overline{X})(Y - \overline{Y})/(N - 1)$ —a reflection of average joint variability of pairs of scores around their respective means—and given that covariance of a *single* set of scores equals $\Sigma(Y - \overline{Y})(Y - \overline{Y})/(N - 1) = S^2$, one could determine all treatment variances and all possible covariances and place them in an array, called a *variance-covariance matrix*:

	J_1	J_2	J_3	J_4
J_1	S^2	S_{ij}	S_{ij}	S_{ij}
J_2	S_{ij}	S^2	S_{ij}	S_{ij}
J_3	S_{ij}	S_{ij}	S^2	S_{ij}
J_4	S_{ij}	S_{ij}	S_{ij}	S^2

The variances of each treatment level are along the diagonal and were assumed to be equal. The covariances of each pair of treatment levels $(J_1J_2, J_1J_3,$ etc.) are along the off-diagonal and also were assumed to be equal. Such an array or matrix, with equal variances and covariances, is said to have compound symmetry or to be a *type S matrix* (Huynh & Feldt, 1970). Such a matrix, too, could be true only of an additive model. If subject and treatment effects interact, the covariances could not be assumed to be equal across all treatment combinations.

In 1954, Box demonstrated that if the population variance-covariance matrix from repeated measures taken on a single group of individuals does not have a pattern that yields an F ratio that is distributed as F, the calculated value is not part of such a distribution with $(J - 1)$ and $(J - 1)(n_j - 1)$ degrees of freedom. (In 1962 Imhof came to a similar conclusion.) Instead, it belongs to an F distribution with $\varepsilon(J - 1)$ and $\varepsilon(J - 1)(n_j - 1)$ degrees of freedom (when treatment has no effect). Box further showed that the upper bound of ε is 1.00 with no deviation from the pattern, but is lower depending on the extent of deviation. Initially that pattern was assumed to be compound symmetry (e.g., Romaniuk, Levin, & Hubert, 1977). The implication is that if there are consistent shifts in performance (i.e., covariances are equal), then $(J - 1) = \varepsilon(J - 1)$ and $(J - 1)(n_j - 1) = \varepsilon(J - 1)(n_j - 1)$. However, if compound symmetry is violated, $(J - 1) > \varepsilon(J - 1)$ and $(J - 1)(n_j - 1) > \varepsilon(J - 1)(n_j - 1)$. If one then evaluates the F ratio with the usual number of degrees of freedom, the critical F value actually is *smaller* than it should be for a legitimate test and could result in rejection of a null hypothesis that should have been retained (i.e., there would be too many type I errors committed). The tabled value is too small (because of inflated degrees of freedom) and erroneously can lead to rejection of the null hypothesis. Box proposed an adjustment to be made on the numerator and denominator degrees of freedom, by a factor equal to ε, that would reduce the occurrence of the type I error and lead to a more valid test of the null hypothesis.

Geisser and Greenhouse (1958) extended Box's analysis to a split-plot (two-factor) design and showed that the lower bound of ε is $1/(J - 1)$, so that (in view of the limited access to computers at that time) a simpler, but admittedly more conservative, test could employ degrees of freedom of $1/(J - 1) \times (J - 1) = 1$, and $1/(J - 1) \times (J - 1)(n_j - 1) = (n_j - 1)$ when ε does not equal 1.00. This, too, was taken as a lack of compound symmetry. However, more recent work revealed that although compound symmetry is a sufficient condition for conducting the F test, it is not a necessary assumption.

Sphericity or Circularity. In 1970, Huynh and Feldt and Rouanet and Lépine independently demonstrated that a necessary and sufficient condition for conducting the repeated measures analysis, without correction applied to degrees of freedom, is that all differences between pairs of scores be equally variable. If a variance-covariance matrix were to be constructed, although it might not reveal compound symmetry, it could demonstrate equal variances of differences between pairs of scores. Such a matrix was called an *H matrix* by Huynh and Feldt and was said to have the property of *sphericity*; Rouanet and Lépine referred to the property as *circularity*. However, matrices that demonstrate compound symmetry also have the property of *sphericity*. Compound symmetry is a special case of sphericity, but the latter is less restrictive than compound symmetry. Whereas compound symmetry requires $\{1/2[J(J + 1)]\} - 2$ equalities (of both variances and covariances), sphericity requires only $\{1/2[J(J - 1)]\} - 1$ equalities (only of variances of differences; Rouanet and Lépine, 1970).

In order to understand this assumption, consider the definition of variance of differences between pairs of scores:

$$\sigma_{y-y}^2 = \sigma_1^2 + \sigma_2^2 - 2\sigma_{12}$$

where

σ_1^2	= variance of one set of scores,
σ_2^2	= variance of the paired set of scores, and
σ_{12}	= covariance, as defined earlier.

Sphericity requires that variances of differences for all treatment combinations be homogeneous (i.e., $\sigma_{y1-y2}^2 = \sigma_{y2-y3}^2$, etc.). These variances can be estimated in one of two ways. One way is to determine estimates of σ_1^2, σ_2^2, and σ_{12}. Consider the fixed-ratio levels of data in Table 3.1, reproduced below:

	A	$(Y_{i1} - \overline{Y}_j)$	B	$(Y_{i2} - \overline{Y}_j)$	A − B
	10	3	19	7	−9
	9	2	13	1	−4
	4	−3	10	−2	−6
	5	−2	6	−6	−1
$\overline{Y}_j =$	7.0		12.0		

The variances are 8.67 for the A and 30.0 for the B condition. Covariance is 13.67, and $S_{y1-y2}^2 = 8.67 + 30 - 2(13.67) = 11.33$.

The second, more direct way of determining variance of the difference is to calculate the difference between scores of two treatment levels (e.g., A – B) and determine the variance of these differences. The differences between the scores are in the last column and the variance of these differences is 11.33. Similar variances would be found for A – C, A – D, B – C, B – D, and C – D scores. The assumption is that all of these variances are homogeneous.

In terms of multivariate analyses, sphericity is said to exist if the following identity holds true:

$$C' \Sigma C = \tau I.$$

Here, C is a matrix of $(J - 1)$ independent or orthogonal contrasts among means that have been normalized (orthonormal contrasts), Σ is the population variance-covariance matrix, C' is the transpose of C, τ is a constant, and I is an identity matrix with 1.00s on the diagonal and 0s along the off-diagonal. If $\tau = \sigma^2$, then $C'\Sigma C$ equals a matrix with σ^2 along the diagonal and 0s along the off-diagonal.

The starting point is a set of the $(J - 1)$ orthogonal contrasts to be conducted among the various treatment means. These may take the following form for the data of Table 3.1:

$$
\begin{array}{c|ccc}
J & C_1 & C_2 & C_3 \\
\hline
A & 1 & 1 & 1 \\
B & -1 & 1 & 1 \\
C & 0 & -2 & 1 \\
D & 0 & 0 & -3
\end{array}
$$

The first contrast (C_1) compares mean rates of responding under fixed ratios of A with B (i.e., do those two means differ), the second (C_2) compares mean rates of responding under fixed ratios of A and B with C (i.e., do the collective means of A and B differ from C), and the third (C_3) compares mean rates of responding under fixed ratios A, B, and C with D. All three contrasts are orthogonal or independent; they provide unique information about differences in rate of responding under the different fixed ratios.

Next, the contrasts are normalized by multiplying each coefficient of a contrast by a value such that the sum of the squared new coefficients = 1.00. If the coefficients of the first contrast, C_1, are squared and summed, $(-1)^2 + (1)^2 = 2.00$. This contrast would be normalized by multiplying each coefficient by $1/\sqrt{2}$: $(-1/\sqrt{2})^2 + (1/\sqrt{2})^2 = 1.00$. For C_2, $(1)^2 + (1)^2 + (-2)^2 = 6.00$, and if each coefficient is multiplied by $1/\sqrt{6}$, then $(1/\sqrt{6})^2 + (1/\sqrt{6})^2 + (-2/\sqrt{6})^2 = 1.00$. Finally, for C_3, $(1)^2 + (1)^2 + (1)^2 + (-3)^2 = 12$ and if each coefficient is multiplied by $1/\sqrt{12}$ then $(1/\sqrt{12})^2 + (1/\sqrt{12})^2 + (1/\sqrt{12})^2 + (-3/\sqrt{12})^2 = 1.00$. The new set of normalized and orthogonal contrasts are said to be ortho-normal. The resulting values may be converted to decimal form and placed in a matrix. For example, $(1/\sqrt{2}) = .707$. Such is the C in the above definition of sphericity, a matrix of orthonomal contrasts:

$$C = \begin{bmatrix} .707 & .408 & .289 \\ -.707 & .408 & .289 \\ 0 & -.816 & .289 \\ 0 & 0 & -.866 \end{bmatrix}$$

The Σ may be estimated from the variances and covariances of the sample data in Table 3.1, and the transpose of C involves interchanging rows and columns of C. Next, the product of $C'\Sigma C$ is determined (cf. Namboodiri, 1984).

Although the strict assumption of compound symmetry is sufficient for performing the F test, it is not necessary. Moreover, sphericity and compound symmetry are tested differently. Nonetheless, the emphasis is on homogeneity of variance of differences, and if the assumption is met, then $MS_A/MS_{res} = F$ may be compared with the tabled value with the appropriate number of df.

As it happens, such homogeneity among variances of differences is a rare occurrence in studies involving more than two repeated measurements of behavior. (When $J = 2$, there is only one covariance and homogeneity must exist.) The effect of going from one treatment level to another is hardly identical for different pairs of treatments. Situations frequently involving repeated measures are longitudinal studies and pretest-treatment-posttest studies. In the former, consecutive measures are more highly correlated than those separated in time (McCall & Applebaum, 1973). In the latter, treatment effects impact differently on subjects and destroy equality among variances of differences (Jaccard & Ackerman, 1985). To the extent that these effects are not identical, variances of differences are unequal, and a comparison of the obtained F with the tabled value is not valid. Instead, the correction proposed by Box and used to compensate for lack of compound symmetry was extended to compensate for lack of sphericity. The adjustment is $\hat{\epsilon}$, epsilon, and ranges from 1 to $1/(J-1)$.

Adjusted Degrees of Freedom

The measure of departure from sphericity, proposed by Box (1954) and extended by Geisser and Greenhouse (1958) to a split-plot design is defined by $\hat{\varepsilon}$ and may be determined by matrix algebra to yield its multivariate form, or it may be arrived at in nonmatrix form. (Actually, it can be determined by a simple command in such computer programs as SPSS and SAS.) In order to facilitate this determination, a matrix of variances and covariances derived from the data of Table 3.1 is presented in Table 3.3. Entries along the diagonal (8.67, 30, 44.67, 40.67) represent the variances for estimations of A, B, C, and D, respectively. Entries on the off-diagonals are covariances. The covariance for A and B (or B and A) is 13.67. That for D and C is 37.67, and so forth. Epsilon depends on the sums and means of the variances and covariances. It is determined by the following equation:

$$\hat{\varepsilon} = \frac{J^2 (\overline{D} - \overline{\mathrm{Cov}_T})^2}{(J-1)(\sum \mathrm{Cov}_{ij}^2 - 2J \sum \overline{\mathrm{Cov}_{i.}^2} + J^2 \overline{\mathrm{Cov}_T^2})}$$

where

$\overline{D}$ = mean of variances along the diagonal,

$\overline{\mathrm{Cov}_T}$ = mean of all entries in the matrix,

Cov_{ij}^2 = a squared entry in the matrix, and

$\mathrm{Cov}_{i.}$ = mean of the entries of a row in the matrix.

For the data of Table 3.3,

$\overline{D}$ = (8.67 + 30 + 44.67 + 40.67)/4 = 31.00

$\overline{\mathrm{Cov}_T}$ = (14 + 26.67 + 33 + 31.34)/4 = 26.2525

$\Sigma \mathrm{Cov}_{ij}^2$ = $(8.67^2 + 13.67^2 + \ldots + 37.67^2 + 40.67^2)$ = 12969.52

$\Sigma \overline{\mathrm{Cov}_{i.}^2}$ = $(14^2 + 26.67^2 + 33^2 + 31.34^2)$ = 2978.4845

$$\hat{\varepsilon} = \frac{16(31 - 26.2525)^2}{3[12969.52 - 2(4)2978.4845 + 16(26.2525)^2]} = \frac{16(22.538756)}{3(168.7441)}$$

$$= 0.7124.$$

The closer $\hat{\varepsilon}$ is to 1.00, the more homogeneous are the variances of differences and the greater the extent of sphericity. The obtained $\hat{\varepsilon}$ is .7124. Accordingly, a more valid test of the null hypothesis will be

TABLE 3.3
Variance-Covariance Matrix of Fixed-Ratio Study

	A	B	C	D	$Cov_{i.}$
A	8.67	13.67	15.67	18.00	14.00
B	13.67	30.00	34.00	29.00	26.67
C	15.67	34.00	44.67	37.67	33.00
D	18.00	29.00	37.67	40.67	31.34

made by reducing numerator and denominator degrees of freedom by a factor of .7124.

For the data of Table 3.1, the original degrees of freedom were 3 and 9, and the critical $F_{(05)}$ = 3.86. The corrected degrees of freedom are 3(.7124) = 2.1 and 9(.7124) = 6.41, and the critical $F_{(05)}$ is between 5.14 and 4.74.

Now, it has been reported (Barcikowski & Robey, 1983; Huynh, 1978; Huynh & Feldt, 1976) that if $\varepsilon > .75$, then an adjustment of df by $\hat{\varepsilon}$ results in too conservative a test (i.e., too many false H_0s fail to be rejected). In fact, it is too conservative when ε is as high as .90 (Collier, Baker, Mandeville, & Hayes, 1967). Therefore, Huynh and Feldt (1976) recommended a less conservative estimation, $\tilde{\varepsilon}$, by

$$\tilde{\varepsilon} = [N(J-1)\hat{\varepsilon}] - 2/(J-1)[N-g-(J-1)\hat{\varepsilon}]$$

where

N	= total number of subjects,
J	= number of treatment conditions, and
g	= number of groups, or 1 for a single-factor study.

Although $\tilde{\varepsilon}$ cannot be estimated with the present data (its value is > 1.00) because of the small number of subjects relative to the number of treatment conditions, it tends to result in a less conservative estimation of ε (i.e., in a larger value).

Although the computer calculation of the Box adjustment is no chore, hand calculation is tedious. Therefore Greenhouse and Geisser (1959) recommended some preliminary examination. Because ε ranges from 1 to $1/(J-1)$, the lowest number of degrees you can use to perform the F test is $(J-1) \times 1/(J-1) = 1$ df for MS_A, and

$(J - 1)(n_j - 1) \times 1/(J - 1) = (n_j - 1)$ df for MS_{res}. For the present study, these dfs would be 1 and $4 - 1 = 3$, and the critical $F_{(05)}$ would be 10.13. The preliminary steps are as follows:

1. Compare the obtained F ratio with the tabled value corresponding to $(J - 1)$ and $(J - 1)(n_j - 1)$ df. If it is not greater than this most liberal value, stop at this point. It will not be significant when degrees of freedom are reduced.
2. If the obtained F ratio is significantly higher than the most liberal value, enter the table with 1 and $(n_j - 1)$ df. If the obtained F is greater than this most conservative value, it is significant. Stop at this point.
3. If the obtained F ratio is higher than the tabled value for df = $(J - 1)$ and $(J - 1)(n_j - 1)$, but lower than the tabled value for df = 1 and $(n_j - 1)$, then the Box adjustment should be applied.

In summary, with the data of Table 3.1, if F is higher than 10.13 it is significant. Indeed, the obtained F was 35.967. If it had been between 10.13 and 3.86, the Box adjustment would have been applied to determine the exact value of the critical $F_{(05)}$. As noted, the critical F would be between 5.14 and 4.74. The obtained F ratio should exceed that new value to be considered significant.

Others (e.g., Jaccard & Ackerman, 1985) have suggested that Box's $\hat{\varepsilon}$ is too conservative and that Huynh's $\tilde{\varepsilon}$ is the most satisfactory correction when the Greenhouse-Geisser three-step strategy warrants an estimation of it. On the other hand, Collier et al. (1967) found reasonable congruence between test size (i.e., estimations of probability of a type I error generated by Monte Carlo studies) and nominal αs (.10, .05, .025, .01) with varying departures from sphericity with the Box correction, more so for sample sizes of 15 than 5. On the basis of these differences in views, a series of recommendations have been made by Barcikowski and Robey (1983). Although stated in terms of ε, in actual practice they refer to calculated estimations of ε.

1. If $\varepsilon > .75$, adjust df by $\tilde{\varepsilon}$.
2. If $\varepsilon < .75$, adjust df by the more conservative $\hat{\varepsilon}$.
3. If nothing is known about ε, adjust df by the conservative $\hat{\varepsilon}$.

Trend Analysis

Because the levels of the independent variable in the present example are quantitative (as opposed to categorical), the data could have been examined in another univariate way. Rather than determining whether mean rates of responding differ, under the circularity assumption, we could determine the simplest trend that describes the changes in rates of responding as the progressive fixed ratios increase. If successive rates of responding increase at the same rate (those at higher fixed ratios are proportionately higher), this would be evidence of a linear trend (i.e., the linear component of the SS_A would be significant). On the other hand, the slope might change as the fixed ratio increases, evidence of a quadratic (second-order) trend. If the slope changes twice, it would suggest a cubic (third-order) trend. In the present case, the simplest trend would depend on the most substantial component of SS_A. In essence, the SS_A and SS_{res} are partitioned into $J - 1$ orthogonal components. Each corresponds to a polynomial, an algebraic expression with at least two terms. One expression corresponds to a linear component, a second corresponds to a quadratic component, and so forth. When the means are weighted by specially derived coefficients (polynomial coefficients), they yield contrasts that are orthogonal—that is, the contrast that reveals the linear component is independent of the one that reveals the quadratic component, and so on.

For these data, obtained from a standard table, the orthogonal polynomials of the linear, quadratic, and cubic components are as follows:

$$
\begin{array}{rrrr}
-3 & 1 & 1 & 3 \\
1 & -1 & -1 & 1 \\
-1 & 3 & -3 & 1
\end{array}
$$

The results of the trend analysis are in Table 3.4. As is evident, the linear and cubic trends are significant. However, the linear SS is 649.8 and accounts for $649.8/683 \times 100 = 95.14\%$ of variability among rate of responding entries. The cubic SS is 24.2 and accounts for $24.2/683 \times 100 = 3.54\%$ of variability. Therefore the relationship between rate of responding and size of fixed ratio is best described as being linear.

Multivariate Approach

Another alternative to a univariate analysis of data of a repeated measures exploratory study, when sphericity has been violated, is to perform a multivariate analysis (MANOVA; e.g., Hotelling's T^2);

TABLE 3.4
Trend Analysis of Fixed-Ratio Data

Source	SS	df	MS	F
Linear	649.8	1	649.8	78.01**
Residual	25	3	8.33	
Quadratic	9	1	9	1.00
Residual	27	3	9	
Cubic	24.2	1	24.2	14.49*
Residual	5	3	1.67	
Total Source	683	3		
Residual	57	9		

*$p < .05$; **$p < .01$.

sphericity is not an assumption here. In the approach, the original scores are changed into new variables.

This transformation can be one of several types, so long as there are only $J - 1$. One type transforms the J set of scores to $J - 1$ differences. The analysis then is performed on these differences (new variables). A second transformation first involves creating a matrix of orthonormal coefficients (defined earlier), weighting each score by its orthonormal coefficient, and then performing the analysis on these transformed variables. Each analysis will produce the same results (Stevens, 1986). The second transformation will serve as an illustration. A set of $J - 1$ new variables is created by weighting the set of scores of Table 3.1 by the orthonormal contrasts. The contrasts and set of scores are shown below:

J	C_1	C_2	C_3	A	B	C	D
A	.707	.408	.289	10	19	27	28
B	-.707	.408	.289	9	13	25	29
C	0	-.816	.289	4	10	20	18
D	0	0	-.866	5	6	12	17

The first contrast, C_1, specifies that .707 weight each score in the A set, that -.707 weight each score in the B set, and 0 weight each score in the C and D sets. Then, for the first subject, the comparison between

TABLE 3.5
Summary of New Variables Created by Weighting Raw Scores by
Orthonormal Coefficients

	$C_1(A$ vs. $B)$	$C_2[(A + B)$ vs. $C]$	$C_3[(A + B + C)$ vs. $D]$	
	−6.363	−10.200	−8.064	
	−2.828	−11.424	−11.531	
	−4.242	−10.608	−5.762	
	−0.707	−5.304	−8.075	
$\overline{Y}_j =$	−3.535	−9.384	−8.358	
$S^2 =$	5.6650	7.6573	5.6579	$3(\Sigma S^2) = 56.9406$
$n_j(\overline{Y}_j)^2 =$	49.985	352.238	279.425	$= 681.648$
$F =$	8.823	46.000	49.387	

A and B estimations yields the new variable: $.707(10) + -.707(19) + 0(27) + 0(28) = -6.363$. The same transformation is performed for the remaining scores of the next three subjects. The second contrast, C_2, specifies that the A and B estimations be weighted by .408, the C scores be weighted by −.816, and the D scores be weighted by 0. The first subject's second new variable is $.408(10) + .408(19) + -.816(27) + 0(28) = -10.2$. The same general procedure creates the new variable specified by C_3, all of which are summarized in Table 3.5.

Hotelling's T^2 involves matrix algebra and is determined by

$$T^2 = n(\text{row vector of means}) \; S_d^{-1}(\text{column vector of means})$$

where S_d^{-1} is the inverse of the variance-covariance matrix, based on the new scores. Ordinarily these operations are performed by computer.

$$T^2 = 4[-3.535 \; -9.384 \; -8.358] \begin{bmatrix} 5.6650 & 4.4230 & -1.3699 \\ 4.4230 & 7.6573 & 1.4034 \\ -1.3699 & 1.4034 & 5.6579 \end{bmatrix}^{-1} \begin{bmatrix} -3.535 \\ -9.384 \\ -8.358 \end{bmatrix}$$

$$= [-14.14 \; -37.536 \; -33.432] \begin{bmatrix} .4485 & -.2922 & .1811 \\ -.2922 & .3272 & -.1519 \\ .1811 & -.1519 & .2583 \end{bmatrix} \begin{bmatrix} -3.535 \\ -9.384 \\ -8.358 \end{bmatrix}$$

$$= 79.7978$$

T^2 may be converted to F by

$$F = \frac{n_j - J + 1}{(n_j - 1)(J - 1)} \, T^2 = \frac{4 - 4 + 1}{(4 - 1)(4 - 1)} (79.7978) = 8.866.$$

With df = $(J - 1)$ and $(n_j - J + 1) = (4 - 1) = 3$ and $(4 - 4 + 1) = 1$, the F value does not reach significance, in part because $n_j = J$, and the degrees of freedom are less than those for the univariate test.

In the case of the multivariate analysis, because contrasts are independent, the correlations between the new variables will be very low; at least, none will be produced by the transformation. Thus the analysis can be conducted without having to assume sphericity of the variance-covariance matrix, although data are assumed to be multivariate normal and the number of subjects should be larger than the number of treatment levels (cf. Bray & Maxwell, 1985). Moreover, Hotelling's T^2 is but one of the several possible multivariate tests to use. Others are available that differ in power and robustness depending on differences in population mean vectors (Olson, 1976). A step-by-step procedure for conducting a MANOVA on repeated measures data is presented by O'Brien and Kaiser (1985).

Parenthetically, SPSS-X, via a subcommand, routinely will transform scores to orthonormal contrasts when analyzing data of a repeated measures study. The transformed scores then are analyzed by several multivariate tests, in addition to the univariate procedure. In this, each contrast first is analyzed. For example, consider C_1, between the A and B conditions. The mean was −3.535. When this is squared and weighted by the four scores, the result $[4(-3.535)^2 = 49.985]$ is a treatment SS with 1 df. The error for this F ratio is S^2 (5.6650). The analysis of the second contrast, which pitted the A and B conditions against the C condition, has a treatment SS = $4(-9.384)^2 = 352.238$, with 1 df and $MS_{error} = S^2 = 7.6573$. The analysis of the third contrast, the first three versus the last condition, has a treatment SS = $4(-8.358)^2 = 279.425$, with 1 df and $MS_{error} = S^2 = 5.6579$. The univariate analysis includes the sum of the three separate treatment SSs, approximately 683 as was obtained; $SS_{error} = [3(\Sigma S^2)]$, which adds up to 57, again the value obtained in the original analysis.

ANOVA Versus MANOVA

Recent studies suggest that there is no clear advantage to either the univariate or multivariate approach. Indeed, for some sets of data the univariate approach is more powerful, whereas in other instances, with sphericity violated, the multivariate approach may be more powerful (Romaniuk et al., 1977).

Preliminary tests (e.g., by John, described in Grieve, 1984; and by Mauchley, described in Grieve, 1984, and Kirk, 1982) are available to determine whether the sphericity assumption is tenable. Whereas some favor preliminary analysis prior to the univariate ANOVA (e.g., Huynh & Mandeville, 1979), most do not. They are unduly sensitive to departures from normality and result in too many type I errors. In fact, Keselman, Mendoza, Rogan, and Breen (1980) found evidence that sphericity (tested by Mauchley) almost always is violated and recommend that the three-step procedure of Greenhouse and Geisser be followed before applying the $\hat{\varepsilon}$ or $\tilde{\varepsilon}$ adjustment to degrees of freedom. However, unless calculations are done by hand, this procedure is not necessary; computer printouts supply both adjustments.

Nonetheless, the univariate approach is more powerful than a multivariate analysis when variances are homogeneous, because (unadjusted) df associated with the error term are higher than that for Hotelling's T^2. However, if variability is great, small effects may be hidden by the univariate test, in which case the multivariate approach is more powerful. But multivariate analysis would not be appropriate if $(n_j - 1) < J$; the variance-covariance matrix is singular (it has no inverse) and no solution is possible (Greenhouse & Geisser, 1959). In view of the differences in views and paucity of clear-cut situations that call for ANOVA or MANOVA, the following has been recommended for analyzing data of an exploratory study (Barcikowski & Robey, 1983):

1. Perform the univariate and a multivariate analysis, each tested at $\alpha_{FW}/2$ level of significance. If the risk of a type I error (falsely rejecting the null hypothesis) for at least one test in a group of tests, familywise α, is set at .05, each F test is performed at the .025 level of significance.
2. The univariate test should be performed with adjusted degrees of freedom as described earlier—that is, corrected by $\hat{\varepsilon}$ when $\varepsilon < .75$ or is unknown, and by $\tilde{\varepsilon}$ when $\varepsilon > .75$.

Analyses of Means Differences

Planned Comparisons. Detection of precise means differences is part of any analysis of experimental results. If precise differences are anticipated a priori, means comparisons can be planned and conducted without the omnibus F test. Generally, researchers have used MS_{res} as the error term for each comparison without regard to the circularity assumption. However, this is only appropriate if $\varepsilon \approx 1.00$. As is clear by now, this assumption hardly is tenable because individual-by-treatment interaction usually occurs. As a result, variances of the contrasts differ, and use of a common MS_{res} may result in an incorrect conclusion. Therefore, it is recommended that separate error terms be employed for each comparison (Keselman, 1982; Keselman, Rogan, & Games, 1981; Mitzel & Games, 1981). In effect, each comparison is conducted as though it were a separate experiment with as many scores as are in the treatment levels being compared. Each would employ the MS_{res} calculated for that set of data. If the comparisons are orthogonal, a popular procedure (cf. Hayes, 1988; Keppel, 1982; Kirk, 1982) is to conduct each test at the .05 level, but with df appropriate for the number of scores in the comparisons. For example, you might predict that one would work harder if the price of food skyrocketed as compared with a slight increase in cost. This could involve a comparison between rates of responding under fixed ratios of 5:1 and 10:1 versus 15:1 and 20:1. Another prediction might be that an increase in the price of food that is already costly also would result in an increase in work to buy it. This would involve a comparison between rates of responding under a fixed ratio of 15:1 versus 20:1. As mentioned, orthogonal comparisons on transformed scores are routinely performed by the SPSS-X MANOVA program for repeated measures; each one performed with a separate error term, as seen in Table 3.5.

If the tests are not orthogonal, then the alpha level used for each comparison, α_{pc}, requires adjustment to protect the overall familywise probability of the type I error. This is because comparisons are not independent; they contain overlapping information and what affects one comparison outcome can easily affect another comparison outcome. The modified Bonferroni approach suggested by Keppel (1982) seems reasonable. Accordingly, if the number of planned comparisons equals $J - 1$, then no adjustment in α_{pc} is made. Each test, for example, could be conducted at the .05 level. If there are four levels and three comparisons are planned, then the α_{fw} will be 3(.05) = .15. However, if the number of planned comparisons exceeds $J - 1$, then an adjustment in α is introduced: The familywise error rate for $J - 1$ comparisons would be divided by the number of comparisons actually planned. If that number is 4, for example, then the α_{pc} = .15/4 = .0375.

Post Hoc Pairwise Comparisons. The same procedure is recommended for pairwise comparisons, when the omnibus F ratio is significant. Although some maintain that circularity does not apply to situations with 1 df (e.g., Edwards, 1985; Rogan, Keselman, & Mendoza, 1979), it does apply if each comparison uses the same MS_{res}. Mitzel and Games (1981) showed that when $\varepsilon = 1.00$ (i.e., the sphericity assumption has been met), there is little loss in power when the overall MS_{res} is used, versus separate error terms for each comparison, especially with large samples. But, when $\varepsilon < 1.00$ the use of MS_{res} results in nonsignificant differences between two means that are declared significant (too lenient a type I error rate) or in undetected differences (too conservative a type I error rate). As a result, it is recommended that separate error terms be calculated for each comparison (Keselman, 1982; Keselman et al., 1981; Mitzel & Games, 1981).

Identical analyses would be conducted on a smaller scale, but with an adjusted α_{pc} and reduced df because fewer scores are being analyzed. As an example, we'll compare rates of responding under fixed ratios A and B. This is identical to conducting the first comparison of Table 3.5. The relevant data are in Table 3.6.

$$SS_T = 888 - (28 + 48)^2/8 \qquad = 166$$

$$SS_A = 4[(7 - 9.5)^2 + (12 - 9.5)^2] \qquad = 50$$

$$SS_S = 2[(14.5 - 9.5)^2 + \ldots + (5.5 - 9.5)^2] \qquad = 99$$

$$SS_{res} = 166 - (50 + 99) \qquad = 17$$

$MS_A = 50/1 = 50$; $MS_{res} = 17/(1)(3) = 5.67$; $F = 50/5.67 = 8.82$; and with df = 1 and 3, $p > .05$. This comparison results in a nonsignificant difference, the same found for the first comparison in Table 3.5. It suggests that the pigeons do not work harder when the cost of food increases from a low to a somewhat higher price (requiring 10 responses per access to food versus 5 responses for the same access). If the analysis had been conducted with the overall MS_{res} as error, the F ratio would be $50/6.33 = 7.90$ with 1 and 9 df. There are 6 possible pairwise comparisons among the four means, and if the Bonferroni approach is used, the F still would not be significant at $\alpha_{pc} = .05/6 = .008$.

Similar analyses performed on the remaining pairs of scores yielded the following results. The comparisons between A and C, A

TABLE 3.6
Rate-of-Responding Data for a Two-Means Comparison

Subjects	5	10	$\overline{Y}_i$
1	10	19	14.5
2	9	13	11
3	4	10	7
4	5	6	5.5
$\Sigma Y =$	28	48	—
$\Sigma Y_2 =$	222	666	888
$\overline{Y}_j =$	7.0	12.0	9.5

and D, B and C, and B and D all yielded significant F ratios; that between C and D was not significant. It generally shows that discernible increases in the cost of food does result in higher rates of responding (i.e., harder work for food).

Other comparisons might be made on a post hoc basis following a significant omnibus F test. A Scheffé test is suitable if nonsimple comparisons involving collective means are desirable (e.g., means A and B versus C and D). If only pairwise comparisons are to be made, the Bonferroni approach, with separate error terms and $(n_j - 1)$ df, has been recommended with $\alpha_{pc} = 2\alpha_{FW}/J(J - 1)$, or α_{FW}/#comps. Maxwell (1980) found this to be most robust in maintaining a type I error rate of about .05 under varying departures from circularity, with sample sizes of 8 or 15, and three to five levels of the repeated measures factor. In our example, all six pairwise comparisons would be conducted with 1 and 3 df, and significant differences declared when $p \leq$ .05/6 = .008. The often recommended Tukey test, on the other hand, resulted in inflated αs even with separate error terms for each comparison and df = $n_j - 1$.

Strength of Association
Between Independent and Response Variables

As is true of any analysis of variance that yields a significant F ratio, it is useful to estimate the extent to which total variability in measurements can be attributed to the treatment or independent variable. In this instance such a determination would yield the extent to which variability in rate of responding is associated with the fixed ratios. This estimation involves some ratio between treatment-related variability to total sources of variability. One of the most popular is an estimation of ω^2, omega square (Hayes, 1988). The solution is straightforward for studies involving independent groups, but is troublesome when repeated measures are involved, depending on the assumptions underlying the test. If one assumes an additive model, there is no problem. Total variability is the sum of variability due to treatment, the subject, and random error. Then ω^2 is estimated by

$$\frac{SS_{tr} - (J - 1)MS_e}{SS_T + MS_S}.$$

However, the usual assumption is a nonadditive or interaction model in which total variability additionally is due to the subject by treatment interaction. The problem this presents is that when each source of variability is estimated and all sources are added together to form the denominator of the ratio, their sum is greater than total variability. The net result is that ω^2 will be slightly underestimated. You can choose to ignore the slight loss in accuracy (which we shall do), determine whether an assumption of additivity is justified, or, as suggested by Dodd and Schultz (1973), replicate the repeated measures sufficiently so that it is possible to determine MS_e directly and yield an accurate total variability denominator. Nonetheless, because the underestimation of ω^2 is slight when interaction is assumed, we can choose to overlook it and (from Table 3.2) proceed with the following:

$$\omega^2 = \frac{SS_{tr} - (J - 1)MS_{res}}{SS_T + MS_S + (n_j)MS_{res}} = \frac{683 - (4 - 1)\,6.33}{1055 + 105 + (4)6.33} = 0.56$$

This indicates that approximately 56% of variability in rate of responding (i.e., work) is associated with the size of the fixed ratios (i.e., cost of food).

4. TWO-FACTOR STUDIES
WITH REPEATED MEASURES ON BOTH FACTORS

A second situation involving repeated measures includes two factors, with the advantage that interaction as well as main effects may be determined. This is not a popular design, with the same individuals serving in all treatment combinations, but it has been employed in learning and retention studies. As an example, we will consider a study in retention, modeled after one conducted by Pusen, Erickson, Hue, and Vyas (1988). Retrieval studies often use primes (stimuli, e.g., words) presented before others that require a response. The prime has to be retrieved, with its known characteristics, and compared with the stimulus before a response occurs. For our study the primes are neutral (e.g., asterisks) or words that represent members of a category (e.g., metal). The stimuli are one-sentence definitions of a member of the category.

Each of five individuals will view a prime on a computer monitor, followed by a definition. If the definition matches the prime, the individual is to repeat that word. If it does not match, the individual is required to say "asterisk" (for the neutral prime) or respond with the word actually defined. Therefore, the subject is required to retrieve the prime (and learned related information) and compare it with the definition. The two factors to be varied relate to the nature of the definitions and primes. The definition can be typical of a member of the category (e.g., a type of metal used to make pennies) or it can be low in typicality (e.g., a metal usually found in thermometers). The primes are either correct (e.g., copper), highly typical but incorrect matches with the definition (e.g., gold), low typical but incorrect matches with the definition (e.g., zinc), or neutral. We will be interested in the average number of errors each individual makes over a series of 64 presentations in which the various combinations of definitions and primes are counterbalanced. There are eight combinations and five individuals for a total of 40 scores (2 types of definitions × 4 types of primes × 5 individuals). The research questions of interest are as follows: Will errors be a function of the typicality of the definition? Will errors be a function of the type of prime? And, perhaps most important, will errors be a function of the combined effects of the definition and prime types?

The answers are derived from an analysis of the 40 scores that is based on one of two models. The more powerful additive model assumes no subject-treatment interaction and is represented by

$$Y_{ijk} - \mu = \alpha_j + \beta_k + \pi_i + \alpha\beta_{jk} + \varepsilon_{ijk}.$$

Because this model is justified only if subject interaction can be ruled out statistically (Kirk, 1982), the focus is on the nonadditive model, which assumes such interaction. Moreover, because definition type and prime type both produce constant, fixed effects and individuals are considered a random sample, whose effects are not predictable, the statistical model is for mixed (fixed and random) effects.

Partitioning of Sums of Squares

This analysis also can be approached by determining the factors that enter into the difference between any single score and the grand mean. For the single-factor study there were two main factors: The subject's mean difference from the grand mean (between-subjects) and the subject's score difference from his or her own mean (within-subjects). In this present instance also the within-subjects component is further partitioned. If you ask why a score differs from the individual's own mean, there are six sources: (a) The individual received a particular prime; (b) the individual saw a particular definition; (c) the prime and definition effects may have interacted; (d) the subject effect interacted with the prime type effect; (e) the subject effect interacted with the definition type effect; and (f) the particular subject effect interacted with the prime type effect for a particular definition type. (There is also random, experimental error, but there is no way to estimate it separately.) If these various sources of difference between a score and the grand mean are applied to the population, the parametric statistical model to guide the analysis is

$$Y_{ijk} - \mu = \alpha_j + \beta_k + \pi_i + \alpha\beta_{jk} + \pi\alpha_{ij} + \pi\beta_{ik} + \pi\alpha\beta_{ijk} + \varepsilon_{ijk}.$$

The terms are not really new. Thus,

α_j = fixed effect of the prime type (factor A);

β_k = fixed effect of the definition type (factor B);

π_i = effect of the person;

$\alpha\beta_{jk}$ = interaction effects of the prime and definition;

$\pi\alpha_{ij}$ = interaction effects of the person and prime;

$\pi\beta_{ik}$ = interaction effects of the person and definition;

$\pi\alpha\beta_{ijk}$ = interaction effects of person, prime, and definition; and

ε_{ijk} = random effect of the ith person receiving the jth prime type followed by the kth definition.

When each of these components is estimated, they yield the empirical model that will generate answers to the three basic research questions. For simplicity in reading, $\overline{Y}_{.j.}$ is expressed as $\overline{Y}_j$, $\overline{Y}_{..k}$ as $\overline{Y}_k$, and so on. The fixed (column) effect of a prime ($\mu_{.j.} - \mu$) is estimated by $\overline{Y}_j - \overline{Y}_g$. Likewise, the fixed (row) effect of definition ($\mu_{..k} - \mu$) is estimated by $\overline{Y}_k - \overline{Y}_g$. The random effect of the subject ($\mu_{i..} - \mu$) is estimated by $\overline{Y}_i - \overline{Y}_g$. Of the four interaction components, $\alpha\beta_{jk}$ represents the interaction of prime and definition effects ($\mu_{.jk} - \mu_{.j.} - \mu_{..k} + \mu$) and is estimated by $\overline{Y}_{jk} - \overline{Y}_j - \overline{Y}_k + \overline{Y}_g$. The $\pi\alpha_{ij}$ represents interaction between a particular person and particular prime effect ($\mu_{ij.} - \mu_{.j.} - \mu_{i..} + \mu$) and is estimated by $\overline{Y}_{ij} - \overline{Y}_j - \overline{Y}_i + \overline{Y}_g$. Similarly, $\pi\beta_{ik}$ is interaction between a particular person and a particular definition effect ($\mu_{i.k} - \mu_{..k} - \mu_{i..} + \mu$) and is estimated by $\overline{Y}_{ik} - \overline{Y}_k - \overline{Y}_i + \overline{Y}_g$. Finally, $\pi\alpha\beta_{ijk}$ is the interaction between a person effect and the effect of a particular prime-definition combination. This is the residual of differences between individual scores and their means after all main effects and interaction effects are removed. If each effect is subtracted from ($Y_{ijk} - \mu_i$), what remains is ($Y_{ijk} - \mu_{.jk} - \mu_{ij.} - \mu_{i.k} + \mu_{.j.} + \mu_{..k} + \mu_{i..} - \mu$), which is estimated by $Y_{ijk} - \overline{Y}_{jk} - \overline{Y}_{ij} - \overline{Y}_{ik} + \overline{Y}_j + \overline{Y}_k + \overline{Y}_i - \overline{Y}_g$.

To get a better picture of the analysis, a set of hypothetical data is presented in Table 4.1. First we'll see that the difference between any given score and the grand mean can be partitioned into seven components. The score of the second person who was presented with a correct prime followed by a highly typical definition will be used. The score is 2 and the grand mean of all 40 scores is 9.875. The difference can be partitioned into a between-subjects and a within-subjects component:

$$(Y_{ijk} - \overline{Y}_g) = (\overline{Y}_i - \overline{Y}_g) + (Y_{ijk} - \overline{Y}_i)$$

$$(2 - 9.875) = (8.0 - 9.875) + (2 - 8.0)$$

$$-7.875 = -1.875 + -6.0$$

The individual's mean of 8.0 is based on the sum of the eight scores or the sum of [32 (high) + 32 (low)]/8 = 8.0. The between-subjects

TABLE 4.1
Factorial Study with Repeated Measures on Both Factors

	Subject	Correct	High Typical	Low Typical	Neutral	ΣY_{ik}	$\overline{Y}_i$
High	1	7	10	12	8	37	9.5
	2	2	6	14	10	32	8
	3	5	15	16	8	44	10.75
	4	9	11	15	15	50	10.875
	5	7	13	13	9	42	11
$\overline{Y}_{jk}$		6	11	14	10	10.25	
Low	1	8	19	9	3	39	
	2	7	11	10	4	32	
	3	5	12	12	13	42	
	4	6	13	8	4	31	
	5	4	15	11	16	46	
$\overline{Y}_{jk}$		6	14	10	8	9.25	
$\Sigma Y_T =$		60	125	120	90	395	
$\Sigma Y_T^2 =$		398	1,671	1,500	1,000	4,569	
$\overline{Y}_j =$		6	12.5	12	9	9.875	

component, the difference between the individual's overall mean (of 8.0) and the grand mean, is −1.875. The within-subjects component, the difference between the score and the individual's overall mean, is −6.0. And −1.875 + −6.0 = −7.875. The −6.0 is partitioned into six components:

1. $\text{est}\alpha_j = (\overline{Y}_j - \overline{Y}_g) = (6.0 - 9.875)$ $= -3.875$

2. $\text{est}\beta_k = (\overline{Y}_k - \overline{Y}_g) = (10.25 - 9.875)$ $= 0.375$

3. $\text{est}\alpha\beta_{jk} = (\overline{Y}_{jk} - \overline{Y}_j - \overline{Y}_k + \overline{Y}_g) = (6.0 - 6.0 - 10.25 + 9.875) = -0.375$

4. $\text{est}\pi\alpha_{ij} = (\overline{Y}_{ij} - \overline{Y}_j - \overline{Y}_i + \overline{Y}_g) = (4.50 - 6.0 - 8.0 + 9.875) = 0.375$

5. $\text{est}\pi\beta_{ik} = (\overline{Y}_{ik} - \overline{Y}_k - \overline{Y}_i + \overline{Y}_g) = (8.0 - 10.25 - 8.0 + 9.875) = -0.375$

6. $\text{est}\pi\alpha\beta_{ijk} = (Y_{ijk} - \overline{Y}_{jk} - \overline{Y}_{ij} - \overline{Y}_{ik} + \overline{Y}_j + \overline{Y}_k + \overline{Y}_i - \overline{Y}_g)$

$ = (2.0 - 6.0 - 4.50 - 8.0 + 6.0 + 10.25 + 8.0 - 9.875) \quad = \dfrac{-2.125}{-6.000}$

Note that $\overline{Y}_{ij}$ is the mean of the individual's performance after both types of definitions [i.e., $(2 + 7)/2 = 4.50$], and $\overline{Y}_{ik}$ is that individual's average errors after exposure to the four prime types [i.e., $(2 + 6 + 14 + 10)/4 = 8.0$].

This partitioning of $(Y_{ijk} - \overline{Y}_g)$ would be performed for all 40 scores. When each component is squared and summed, the result is eight separate sums of squared deviations, yielding the following empirical model:

$$SS_T = SS_A + SS_B + SS_S + SS_{A \times B} + SS_{A \times S} + SS_{B \times S} + SS_{A \times B \times S}.$$

Don't lose sight of the information being sought. The intent is to determine whether a particular prime-definition combination will have a differential effect on errors in comparing the prime with a definition—that is, whether the two effects interact. This will stem from $SS_{A \times B}$, and the answer will be supplied by an F ratio. If the answer is no, then the intent is to determine whether the prime types have a main, independent effect on errors. This information will stem from SS_A, and the question will be answered by a second F ratio. If the intent is to determine whether the definition's typicality has a main, independent effect on errors, this information will stem from SS_B, and the answer supplied by a third F ratio.

Calculation of Sums of Squares

Calculations of sums of squares are likely to be performed by computer. The SS for the main effects of factors A (prime) and B (definition) are determined as in the single-factor study. The between-subjects effect proceeds along the same line, keeping in mind that the same five individuals participated in all treatment combinations and that each mean is based on eight scores. The prime × definition interaction SS duplicates that for any two-factor study. Interactions involving the person component require collapsing cells. The person × prime component examines prime effects, ignoring definition, and requires composite

TABLE 4.2
Summary of Analysis of Variance with Repeated Measures on Two
Factors

Source	SS	df	MS	F
Subjects	46.0	4	11.50	
Columns (Prime)	271.875	3	90.625	11.820**
Subject × Prime	92.0	12	7.667	
Rows (Definition)	5.625	1	5.625	0.529
Subject × Definition	42.5	4	10.625	
Prime × Definition	66.875	3	22.292	1.864
Subject × Prime				
× Definition	143.5	12	11.958	
Total	668.375	39		

Multivariate Analyses of Prime Type Effect
    Greenhouse-Geisser Epsilon = 0.72463
    Huynh-Feldt Epsilon = 1.0000
    Lower-Bound Epsilon = 0.33333

Test Name	Value	Exact F	Hypothetical df	Error df	Significance of F
Pillais	0.95937	15.74095	3.000	2.000	.060
Hotellings	23.61143	15.74095	3.000	2.000	.060
Wilks	0.04063	15.74095	3.000	2.000	.060
Roys	0.95937				

**$p < .01$.

scores for each person under each of the four prime types. Similarly, the person × definition interaction ignores prime type and focuses on the composite scores, reflecting errors after high and low typicality definitions (two scores) following all prime types. Finally, the triple interaction SS is residual variability.

Mean Squares and F Ratios

A summary of the entire analysis is in the top portion of Table 4.2. Mean squares are determined by SS/df, with df dependent upon the number of levels of a factor minus one, or the product of degrees of freedom of factors whose effects might interact. The F ratios provide answers to the questions posed originally. They are formed on the basis of the expected long-range, average values of the MSs. Therefore, for a mixed-effects model with prime type and definitions as fixed factors and subjects as the random factor, it is assumed that the subject variable interacts with the independent variables. When this is true, E(MS) will include interaction.

Each of the hypotheses is tested by forming an F ratio such that it will approximately equal 1.00 if there is no effect of treatment or be significantly greater than 1.00 if there is an effect. Based on E(MS)s, each numerator will contain the effect component in addition to the error component. A summary of expected values reveals what these ratios will be for the nonadditive model:

$$E(MS_A) = n_j \sum \alpha^2/(J-1) \qquad + K\sigma_{\pi\alpha}^2 + \sigma_{\varepsilon}^2$$

$$E(MS_{A \times S}) = \qquad\qquad K\sigma_{\pi\alpha}^2 + \sigma_{\varepsilon}^2$$

$$E(MS_B) = n_k \sum \beta^2/(K-1) \qquad + J\sigma_{\pi\beta}^2 + \sigma_{\varepsilon}^2$$

$$E(MS_{B \times S}) = \qquad\qquad J\sigma_{\pi\beta}^2 + \sigma_{\varepsilon}^2$$

$$E(MS_{A \times B}) = n_{jk} \sum\sum \alpha\beta^2/(J-1)(K-1) + \sigma_{\pi\alpha\beta}^2 + \sigma_{\varepsilon}^2$$

$$E(MS_{A \times B \times S}) = \qquad\qquad \sigma_{\pi\alpha\beta}^2 + \sigma_{\varepsilon}^2$$

The first question related to whether the prime types had an effect on errors. The answer stems from an F ratio of $MS_A/MS_{A \times S}$. This yielded $F = 11.820$, which, with 3 and 12 df, is significant. The prime types had a differential effect on errors. The second question asked whether the definition's typicality had an effect on errors. The answer stems from an F ratio of $MS_B/MS_{B \times S}$. This yielded $F = 0.529$, which, with 1 and 4 df, is not significant. The definitions did not have an effect on errors. The last question asked whether the effect of the prime interacted with the effect of the definition. The answer stems from an F ratio of $MS_{A \times B}/MS_{A \times B \times S}$. This yielded an F ratio of 1.864, which, with 3 and 12 df, is not significant and indicates that the effect of a given type of prime on errors does not depend on whether the definition is typical of the category member or is less typical. However, conclusions depend on whether assumptions of the test have been met.

Assumptions of the Factorial Analysis
with Repeated Measures

The assumptions underlying the completely within-subjects design are similar to those of the single-factor study. Thus, scores are assumed to have a multivariate normal distribution and to be independent among individuals; variances and variances of differences are assumed to be homogeneous. This circularity assumption was fully discussed by Rouanet and Lépine (1970), with the completely within-subjects design as an example.

There are two primary cases to consider. First, if an additive model applies, there is no subject × treatment interaction, and it can be assumed that $\sigma^2_{\pi\alpha} = \sigma^2_{\pi\beta} = \sigma^2_{\pi\alpha\beta}$. Each partial interaction variance estimates a common overall interaction variance, and a weighted average of these mean squares is a valid error mean square for an overall F test. If this is true, then an overall variance-covariance matrix should satisfy circularity. Such equality of partial interaction variances is a necessary and sufficient condition for validity of the overall F test (Rouanet and Lépine, 1970). The overall matrix includes variances and covariances of *all* treatment combinations. In our example, this would constitute an 8 × 8 matrix (4 levels of A combined with 2 levels of B). Use of the overall variance-covariance matrix to establish circularity is a rigorous test, but if it demonstrates circularity, all three submatrices (corresponding to the main effect of A, B, and interaction) also satisfy the circularity assumption. Each of the three F tests would be valid and may be performed with an error term derived from pooling the three interaction variances ($MS_{A\times S}$, $MS_{B\times S}$, $MS_{A\times B\times S}$). This is a more powerful test because denominator df are increased (here from 12, 4, and 12 to 28). Hence it is worthwhile to test the interaction variances for homogeneity and pool them if they are alike (Edwards, 1985).

The second case is when a nonadditive model is appropriate or the overall variance-covariance matrix does not satisfy the circularity assumption. It is still possible for the submatrices to satisfy the assumption. If they do, valid tests can be performed, but the error MSs are the interaction terms used in the example (i.e., the partial interaction mean squares). These use fewer df in the denominator, but the tests are still powerful; each MS_e is independent and all allowable tests (corresponding to the matrices that satisfy circularity) are independent of each other.

In this instance, as in the single-factor study, a test for circularity is not recommended (Rogan et al., 1979). Instead, if the assumption is not satisfied, as suggested by ε values less than 1.00, the $\hat{\varepsilon}$ or $\tilde{\varepsilon}$ correction for df may be applied directly, or a multivariate analysis could be performed. For the present data, the F ratio of interest is for the main effect of prime type, significant at $p < .01$ with df = 3, 12. The $\hat{\varepsilon}$ equals 0.72463 and corrected df = 0.72463(3) = 2.17 and 0.72463(12) = 8.696. The $F_{(05)} \approx 4.46$, whereas $F_{(025)} \approx 5.71$. The prime type effect is significant and the next step would focus on precise mean differences.

Multivariate Tests

In keeping with a recommendation by Looney and Stanley (1989) for a split-plot design (cf. Chapter 5) of an exploratory study, each effect should be tested by both univariate and multivariate analyses at α = .05/2. The effect is considered significant if $p \leq .025$ for either analysis. Therefore, these data also were analyzed by the multivariate approach. As with the single-factor study, the tests involve extensive matrix algebra. Hence, analyses were performed by computer with SPSS-X (which routinely conducts tests by Pillai, Hotelling, Wilk, and Roy) for each contrast (prime effect, definition effect, interaction). The results of the analyses of the prime effect are shown in the bottom portion of Table 4.2. Notice that this effect was not significant here ($p = .06$) but was with the univariate test ($p < .01$). This illustrates the greater power of univariate testing when near sphericity has been met. On the other hand, interaction clearly was not significant with the univariate test. However $\hat{\varepsilon}$ = .42584 and the multivariate test was more powerful—interaction approached significance with p = .033. Clearly, both approaches should be employed.

Analyses of Mean Differences

In the case of the two-factor study there is the possibility of obtaining main and/or interaction effects. The interaction indicates that conclusions about the main effect may have to be qualified. Particular hypotheses can be tested by planned comparisons, with separate error terms for each single df comparison. The α level of each would depend upon whether the comparisons are orthogonal or nonorthogonal.

Orthogonal comparisons can be tested at, say, $\alpha = .05$. Nonorthogonal ones are tested at lower α levels, on the order of $\alpha_{FW}/\#$ comparisons.

If the omnibus tests are first performed and main effects are significant, further analyses should employ separate appropriate error terms (e.g., separate $MS_{A \times S}$ for column means, reduced df, and α corrected for the familywise error rate). If the interaction effect is significant, its source(s) can be determined by examining simple effects. Whereas the main effect of prime type reflects average effects across types of definitions, simple effects focus on the effect of prime type for each type of definition. With no interaction, each simple effect reflects the same mean differences as do main effect means. Likewise, the main effect of definition type is an average effect for all types of primes, whereas simple effects compare effects of definition type for each kind of prime.

A Bonferroni inequality approach could be applied to tests of simple effects, with the type I error rate set according to each omnibus F test. With $\alpha = .05$, the two-factor study involves three omnibus tests, for an overall $\alpha_{FW} = .15$. If interaction is significant, the analysis of simple effects would be tested at an α equal to the sum of the αs for the main plus interaction effects/# simple effects. For the 2×2 study, the four simple effects would be tested at $\alpha_{pc} = .15/4 = .0375$. For the earlier example, with six simple effects (effect of prime type preceding the two types of definitions and effect of type of definition at each of the four prime types), $\alpha_{pc} = .15/6 = .025$. Unless large effects are predicted, these tests have little power (Keselman & Keselman, 1987). However, not all simple effects may be of interest. Moreover, Holland and Copenhaver (1988) describe several Bonferroni-like procedures that require the exact p value of each test but may increase power by leading to more rejections of H_0 without increasing the probability of a type I error.

For our data, the effect of prime type was significant and was followed by simple comparisons, each using separate error terms (Maxwell, 1980) and $\alpha_{pc} = .025$. These tests are too conservative with so few subjects. Of the six means comparisons, only two were significant. Fewer errors in matching primes with the correct definition were obtained when the prime was correctly defined than when the prime was a highly typical but incorrect member of the category that was defined or when it was a low typical member.

Strength of Association
Between Independent and Response Variables

Few researchers report an estimation of ω^2 for the two-factor repeated measures study; the total sources of variability are very large and unless a sizeable effect is obtained, it is likely to result in a measure of association that is negatively biased and trivial. For the nonadditive model that applied to the present data (Dodd & Schultz, 1973), these sources of variability are

$$SS_T + MS_S + MS_{A \times S} + MS_{B \times S} + n(J + K - 1)MS_{A \times B \times S}.$$

Only the significant main effect is relevant. Thus,

$$\omega^2 = \frac{SS_A - (df)MS_{A \times S}}{SS_T + MS_S + MS_{A \times S} + MS_{B \times S} + n(J + K - 1)MS_{A \times B \times S}}$$

$$= \frac{271.875 - (3)(7.667)}{668.375 + 11.5 + 7.667 + 10.625 + 5(5)11.958} = 0.2496.$$

This suggests that, at a minimum, 24.96% of variability in error scores is accounted for by the nature of the prime that preceded a definition of a member of a category.

5. TWO-FACTOR STUDY WITH REPEATED MEASURES ON ONE FACTOR

The extension of the randomized block factorial study to repeated measures on members of several independent groups is one of the most pervasive designs. For example, several categories of psychoses may be treatable by the same drug, with different effective doses. Rather than $J \times K$ independent groups, you can include the different psychoses and within each group test each individual with all doses. Therefore, the first factor is independent groups, and the second factor is repeated measures on all individuals of each group—a blending of the independent-groups and randomized block design, also known as a *mixed design*. In another example, you might consider a recent concern among social scientists regarding the extent to which male and female teenagers attribute wealth and poverty to different causes.

Gender (factor B) would be manipulated by surveying males and females to form two independent groups, but all teenagers would be measured (repeatedly) on the extent to which four explanations are important (factor A).

In general, if one of the factors is a personality or organismic variable, then that factor (B) only can be varied by selecting independent groups. If the second variable (A) can be introduced quantitatively (e.g., different ages) or qualitatively (e.g., different explanations of poverty) and each individual would not be affected by serving in all conditions (i.e., there are no carry-over effects), then the same individuals can be employed in all conditions. Such mixed designs are not confined to organismic variables as the between-groups factor. Individuals may be randomly assigned to receive one of several treatments (e.g., structured teaching or structured teaching plus computer simulation) and then be measured repeatedly (e.g., on problem solving skills, basic facts, etc.).

When individuals can be randomly assigned to each level of the independent-groups factor, the design generally is called *split-plot*. Mixed design is a broader term. An unsatisfactory feature of this design is that the effect of factor B is confounded by group membership; each group is exposed to or placed in a single level of B and differences in outcome may be due to the level of B per se, the group of persons, or both. The same three research questions can be asked as in the previous design, but the answers are arrived at differently because of the nature of the design. The confounding is taken into account by the use of separate error terms for factors A and B.

Partitioning of Sums of Squares

We will consider an example and partition the SS_T as we did previously. Assume that a group of male and female teenage students at a university were surveyed on the extent to which four explanations of poverty were important: family factors (e.g., family does not stress success), luck (e.g., bad luck), internal factors (e.g., poor money management) , and external factors (e.g., salaries too low). Each explanation or attribution was rated on a scale of 10 (most important) to 70 (not important). This study is based on an extensive one conducted by Stacey, Singer, and Ritchie (1989).

Here, too, the difference between any score and the grand mean can be analyzed. Several factors can be isolated: the score was (a) for a particular explanation of poverty, (b) by a male or female teenager who (c) had a unique effect; (d) the explanation effect may have interacted with the gender effect; and (e) that person may have reacted in a unique way to the particular explanation of poverty. In terms of parameters, the model that guides the analysis is

$$Y_{ijk} - \mu = \alpha_j + \beta_k + \pi_{i(k)} + \alpha\beta_{jk} + \pi\alpha_{i(k)j} + \varepsilon_{ijk}.$$

In this model:

α_j = the fixed effect of attribution, estimated by $(\overline{Y}_j - \overline{Y}_g)$.

β_k = the fixed effect of gender, estimated by $(\overline{Y}_k - \overline{Y}_g)$.

$\pi_{i(k)}$ = the person effect, a form of within-group variability, estimated by $(\overline{Y}_i - \overline{Y}_k)$. The special notation "$(k)$" indicates that persons are nested within levels of the group (gender) factor.

$\alpha\beta_{jk}$ = the interaction of attribution × gender effects, estimated by $(\overline{Y}_{jk} - \overline{Y}_j - \overline{Y}_k + \overline{Y}_g)$.

$\pi\alpha_{i(k)j}$ = the effect of the attribution and unique person combination, for a particular gender, estimated by $(Y_{ijk} - \overline{Y}_{jk} - \overline{Y}_i + \overline{Y}_k)$.

Although the sum of these (squared) estimations reveals the empirical model that will be used, the model is clearer if the total deviation of a score from the grand mean is partitioned to its two main components: between-subjects and within-subjects. The former reflects the difference between a subject's mean and the grand mean. The latter reflects the difference between a subject's score and his or her mean. In summary:

$$(Y_{ijk} - \overline{Y}_g) = (\overline{Y}_i - \overline{Y}_g) + (Y_{ijk} - \overline{Y}_i).$$

Consider the score of 35, for the third female teenager who rated the importance of family factors that contribute to poverty (see Table 5.1). The grand mean is 28.9 and her mean is 25.0. Then,

$$(35 - 28.9) \quad = (25.0 - 28.9) \quad + (35 - 25.0).$$

$$6.1 \quad\quad\quad = -3.9 \quad\quad\quad + 10.$$

TABLE 5.1

Data from a Two-Factor Study with Repeated Measures on One Factor

Factor B	Family	Luck	Internal	External	Sum	$\bar{Y}_i$
			Factor A			
Males	48	31	24	29	132	33.0
	46	34	25	31	136	34.0
	45	37	27	35	144	36.0
	37	39	30	38	144	36.0
	45	34	29	32	140	35.0
$\bar{Y}_{jk}$	44.2	35	27	33		34.8
Females	28	17	19	20	84	21.0
	32	18	20	22	92	23.0
	35	19	22	24	100	25.0
	39	16	19	22	96	24.0
	31	15	20	22	88	22.0
$\bar{Y}_{jk}$	33	17	20	22		23.0
$\bar{Y}_j$	38.6	26	23.5	27.5		28.9

The between- and within-subjects components will not lead to any of the answers being sought; however, their members will.

First, the between-subjects component is considered. Why does a subject's mean rating differ from the grand mean? One reason is that the person was female (or male). Another reason is that her performance shows variability around the group mean, called *subjects-within-group variability*, akin to within-group variability found in any independent-groups design. The first member (group variability) will provide an answer to this question: Is there an independent, average, main effect of gender on rated importance of explanations of poverty? If each of these two members of the between-subjects component of $(Y_{ijk} - \bar{Y}_g)$ are represented along with the numerical values of each term for that score of 35, then,

$$(\bar{Y}_i - \bar{Y}_g) \quad = (\bar{Y}_k - \bar{Y}_g) \quad + (\bar{Y}_i - \bar{Y}_k)$$

$$(25.0 - 28.9) = (23.0 - 28.9) \quad + (25.0 - 23.0)$$

$$-3.9 \quad = -5.9 \quad + 2$$

The second major component of $(Y_{ijk} - \overline{Y}_g)$ is within-subjects variability, the difference between the subject's score and mean. Note the difference between subjects-within-group variability (a member of between-subjects variability) and within-subjects variability. Subjects-within-group variability refers to variablity of subject *means* around each group mean. Within-subjects variability refers to variability of individual *scores* around the individual's mean. In this example, the difference between the individual's score and her mean was 35 – 25 = 10, and we can determine why the teenager's score differs from her mean.

First, she had rated the family-factors explanation of poverty and produced the score of 35. Thus the particular level of the repeated (factor A) is one factor that accounts for the difference. The overall mean for family causes was 38.6 and this $\overline{Y}_j$ differs from the grand mean by $(\overline{Y}_j - \overline{Y}_g) = (38.6 - 28.9) = 9.7$. This member will provide an answer to the question: What is the main, independent, average effect of the different explanations of poverty on their perceived importance? A second factor that may account for within-subjects variability is the combined effects of gender (female) and attribution (family). The mean score for this combination of variables is 33.0. If variability remains after the effects of the group $(\overline{Y}_k)$ and explanation of poverty $(\overline{Y}_j)$ are removed, an interaction effect would be evident. Thus, $(\overline{Y}_{jk} - \overline{Y}_j - \overline{Y}_k + \overline{Y}_g) = (33.0 - 38.6 - 23.0 + 28.9) = 0.30$. This member answers the question: Do the effects of gender and attribution on perceived importance interact?

There is one final reason why a subject's score differs from his or her mean. That particular person, a female, could have reacted in a unique way to the particular explanation. This represents an interaction between the subjects-within-group variability and the importance of attribution, a measure of the extent to which individuals belonging to a particular group are affected equally by each level of the repeated measures variable. This member is estimated by $(Y_{ijk} - \overline{Y}_{jk} - \overline{Y}_i + \overline{Y}_k) = (35.0 - 33.0 - 25.0 + 23.0) = 0$.

The final partitioning has five segments. The deviation of any score from the grand mean consists of two components: between-subjects and within-subjects. The between-subjects component is partitioned into two members: that reflecting group membership and within-group variability. The within-subjects component is partitioned into three members: that reflecting treatment effects (the repeated measures member), group × treatment interaction effects, and treatment × subject-within-group interaction effects. These components and their members are shown with the breakdown for the score of 35 achieved by the third female:

Between-Subjects	Within-Subjects
$(\overline{Y}_i - \overline{Y}_g)$	$+ (Y_{ijk} - \overline{Y}_i)$
$(25 - 28.9)$	$+ (35 - 25)$
-3.9	$+ 10$
$(\overline{Y}_k - \overline{Y}_g) + (\overline{Y}_i - \overline{Y}_k)$	$+ (\overline{Y}_j - \overline{Y}_g) + (\overline{Y}_{jk} - \overline{Y}_j - \overline{Y}_k + \overline{Y}_g)$
	$\quad + (Y_{ijk} - \overline{Y}_{jk} - \overline{Y}_i + \overline{Y}_k)$
$(23 - 28.9) + (25 - 23)$	$+ (38.6 - 28.9) + (33 - 38.6 - 23 + 28.9)$
	$\quad + (35 - 33 - 25 + 23)$
$-5.9 + 2$	$+ 9.7 + 0.3 + 0$

And $(-5.9 + 2 + 9.7 + 0.3) = 6.1 = (Y_{ijk} - \overline{Y}_g) = (35 - 28.9)$.

If the total deviation and each of the members are squared, and the squared deviations summed for all scores of the 10 persons, these sums lead to the empirical model that will guide the analysis:

$$SS_T = SS_B + SS_{swg} + SS_A + SS_{A \times B} + SS_{A \times swg}$$

Computation of Sums of Squares

The rated importance of each explanation for each of the 10 individuals is in Table 5.1. Once again, calculations are most likely to be performed by computer. Just remember that each component of SS_T is based on the estimations of each member, weighted by the number of scores contributing to that member.

Calculation of Mean Squares and *F* Ratios

At this point a summary table is very useful. Table 5.2 (top) is more elaborate than the usual summary table in order to illustrate that $SS_T = SS_{bs} + SS_{ws}$; $SS_{bs} = SS_B + SS_{swg}$; and $SS_{ws} = SS_A + SS_{A \times B} +$

TABLE 5.2

Summary of Analysis of Variance for Two Factors with Repeated Measures on One Factor

Source	SS	df	MS	F
Between-Subjects	1,459.6	9		
Groups (B)	1,392.4	1	1,392.4	165.762
SwithinG	67.2	8	8.4	
Within-Subjects	1,704	30		
Treatment	1,336.2	3	445.4	50.516
Group × Treatment	156.2	3	52.067	5.905
Treatment × SwithinG	211.6	24	8.817	

Multivariate Analyses of Interaction Effects
Greenhouse-Geisser Epsilon = 0.39125
Huynh-Feldt Epsilon = 0.47549
Lower-Bound Epsilon = 0.33333

Test Name	Value	Exact F	Hypothetical df	Error df	Significance of F
Pillais	0.95486	42.30710	3.000	6.000	.000
Hotellings	21.15355	42.30710	3.000	6.000	.000
Wilks	0.04514	42.30710	3.000	6.000	.000
Roys	0.95486				

$SS_{A \times swg}$. The degrees of freedom are determined in the usual way. Thus, $df_B = K - 1$, $df_A = J - 1$, and $df_{A \times B} = (J - 1)(K - 1)$. The df_{swg} warrants some consideration. The SS_{swg} represents the squared differences between each person's mean and the group mean. Because there are $n_{jk} = 5$ means per group and the sum of the deviations of the means from the group mean must equal zero, there is 1 df lost per group, or $df_{swg} = K(n_{jk} - 1) = 2(5 - 1) = 8$. Likewise, because SS_{ws} represents the difference between a person's score and mean, the sum of all J differences must equal zero. Thus 1 df is lost from each set of J deviations, one per subject, or $df_{ws} = N(J - 1) = 10(4 - 1) = 30$. Finally, $df_{A \times swg}$ is the same as that for any interaction, or $df_{A \times swg} = (J - 1)[K(n_{jk} - 1)] = (4 - 1)[2(5 - 1)] = 24$.

The rationale for the F ratios is based on expected mean squares of each component of total variability of the ratings. As shown earlier, the numerator has the added effect component, but is otherwise identical to the denominator. Therefore the ratio should yield approximately 1.00 in the absence of an effect and a value that is significantly greater than 1.00 if there is an effect. What follows is appropriate when both variables yield fixed effects. Accordingly, the following are the long range E(MS)s:

$$E(MS_B) \quad = \sigma_\varepsilon^2 + J\sigma_\pi^2 + nJ\sum \beta^2/(K-1)$$

$$E(MS_{swg}) = \sigma_\varepsilon^2 + J\sigma_\pi^2$$

$$E(MS_A) \quad = \sigma_\varepsilon^2 + \sigma_{\pi\alpha}^2 + nK\sum \alpha^2/(J-1)$$

$$E(MS_{A \times B}) = \sigma_\varepsilon^2 + \sigma_{\pi\alpha}^2 + n_{jk}\sum\sum (\alpha\beta)^2/(J-1)(K-1)$$

$$E(MS_{A \times swg}) = \sigma_\varepsilon^2 + \sigma_{\pi\alpha}^2$$

The appropriate ratio for testing the effect of gender on ratings of importance is $F = MS_B/MS_{swg} = 1,392.4/8.4 = 165.762$. With 1 and 8 df this indicates that the average ratings were higher for females. Note that the df associated with factor B is low, resulting in a much less powerful test than for factor A and interaction. Likewise, the appropriate ratio for testing the effect of the explanations on rated importance is $F = MS_A/MS_{A \times swg} = 445.4/8.817 = 50.516$. With 3 and 24 df this indicates that the various attributions had differential average effects on ratings. Finally, the ratio for testing the interaction effects of group membership and attribution is $F = MS_{A \times B}/MS_{A \times swg} = 52.067/8.817 = 5.905$, which, with 3 and 24 df, is significant and indicates that the effect of attribution depends upon gender. Such would be the conclusion without considering assumptions underlying the tests.

The group factor was treated as a fixed-effect variable. However, organismic variables sometimes are considered as random-effect variables (Edwards, 1985). If factor B is considered as a random sample of females and males, then $E(MS_A) = \sigma_\varepsilon^2 + \sigma_{\pi\alpha}^2 + nK\Sigma\alpha^2/(J-1) + n_{jk}\sigma_{AB}^2$, $E(MS_{AB}) = \sigma_\varepsilon^2 + \sigma_{\pi\alpha}^2 + n_{jk}\sigma_{AB}^2$, and the effect of the repeated measures factor would be evaluated with MS_{AB} as error. Then $F = 445.4/52.067 = 8.554$, and with 3 and 3 df this factor would not be considered significant.

Assumptions Underlying the Mixed Design

The assumptions underlying the two-factor study with repeated measures on one factor are a blending of those of an independent-groups and a single-factor repeated measures design—that is, within-group variability is the same for each of the groups and scores are normally distributed and independent among groups. Should variances be heterogeneous, Looney and Stanley (1989) recommend a more robust test. Brown and Forsythe (1974) describe one by Welch and a modified F^* whose denominator and df are adjusted.

The usual repeated measures assumptions apply to the scores at each level of the group factor (B). In the present example, this means that the population variance-covariance matrices for males and for females are equal and their pooled matrix has a sphericity pattern. Huynh (1978) referred to these two assumptions as *multisample sphericity*. If the assumptions are tenable, the treatment and interaction F tests are valid, using pooled $MS_{A \times swg}$ as the error term. If either assumption is violated, sphericity is untenable. Then, the test for interaction is more vulnerable to a type I error, especially with unequal ns per group (Huynh & Feldt, 1980). Available tests to evaluate the assumptions usually are not recommended. Sphericity almost always is violated and several approaches to handling such data have been investigated.

The approaches vary in robustness (i.e., protection against the type I error and power rate). These include the conservative Greenhouse-Geisser correction, the $\hat{\varepsilon}$ adjustment, the $\tilde{\varepsilon}$ adjustment, and multivariate analysis. (Huynh, in 1978, proposed an improved approximate test and found it to be slightly more robust than the $\tilde{\varepsilon}$ adjustment, but recommended the latter because it requires fewer calculations.) Robustness varies with degree of nonsphericity, normality of the distribution of scores, sample size, and number of levels of the repeated measures factor relative to sample size.

With slight departures from sphericity ($\varepsilon \geq .75$), an adjustment by $\tilde{\varepsilon}$ of degrees of freedom for the repeated measures factor and interaction component is most robust when sample size exceeds the number of levels of the repeated measures factor (Rogan et al., 1979) and in the reverse situation with only two levels of the group factor (Maxwell and Arvey, 1982). With greater departures from sphericity ($\varepsilon < .75$), the $\hat{\varepsilon}$ adjustment has been found to be more robust, especially with more than two groups and moderate sample size (Maxwell & Arvey, 1982), as has multivariate analysis (Rogan et al., 1979), provided that scores are normally distributed.

For the present set of data $\hat{\varepsilon} = .39125$. Adjusted df for the effect of attribution are $.39125(3) = 1.17$ and $.39125(24) = 9.39$. This effect still is significant ($F_{(025)} \approx 7.21$). However, interaction is no longer significant.

Multivariate Analyses

Evidence suggests inconsistency in the extent to which univariate tests or multivariate tests are most suitable when multisample sphericity is violated in an exploratory study. Some investigators recommend use of one of the adjustments on dfs (e.g., Huynh, 1978), others recommend multivariate analysis, especially with large Ns (e.g., McCall & Applebaum, 1973; O'Brien & Kaiser, 1985), whereas others recommend either approach, depending upon parameters of the study (e.g., Maxwell & Arvey, 1982; Rogan et al., 1979). As a reasonable compromise, Looney and Stanley (1989) recommended conducting both analyses. Accordingly, data of this study also were analyzed by MANOVA with $\alpha = .025$. Although Hotelling's T^2 is recommended with two groups and the Pillai-Bartlett test (Pillai, 1955) recommended for more than two groups, the SPSS-X program conducts both.

The results agreed with those of the univariate analysis of main effects. Despite nonsphericity, the effect of attribution was large enough to be evident in the univariate test. Additionally, the multivariate analysis of the interaction effect of gender and attribution was significant. Results are shown in Table 5.2.

Analyses of Means Differences

The choice of the most appropriate procedure to follow in evaluating the effects of an independent variable depends on a number of factors, including the extent to which the sphericity assumption has been met. When sphericity is violated, even small departures from it produce large biases in the F ratios associated with contrasts between means. Compensation for the bias is a function of whether contrasts were planned or are post hoc. A priori tests should be performed with separate, rather than pooled, error terms for testing the effects of the repeated measures variable and partial interactions or simple main effects (both to be explained shortly). These would be accompanied by a reduction in degrees of freedom from $K(n_{jk} - 1)(J - 1)$ to $K(n_{jk} - 1)$ (Boik, 1981).

The general procedures for post hoc testing are more involved.

Tests on Main Effects. Consider the situation in which a main effect is significant and the variable has more than two levels. The group variable (factor B) only requires homogeneous variances among the groups. Therefore comparisons between particular means can employ MS_{swg} as the error term, with $K(n_{jk} - 1)$ degrees of freedom, or separate MS_{swg} terms if the homogeneity assumption is violated. This involves a pooling of within-group variances of the groups being compared and a reduction in degrees of freedom.

The repeated measures factor (A) is tested under the assumption of multisample sphericity, and if the assumption is met $MS_{A \times swg}$ serves as an appropriate error term for these means comparisons, with $(J - 1)[K(n_{jk} - 1)]$ df. If the assumption is not met, separate error terms should be computed for each comparison, consisting of MS_{res} pooled over all groups for the two sets of scores and reduced degrees of freedom. For example, mean ratings of the importance of family contributions to povery versus luck might be compared (from the data in Table 5.1). A single-factor analysis of the data for these two attributions by females yields $MS_{res} = 9.75$, and by males yields $MS_{res} = 24.85$, each with 4 df. The pooled variances, the error term for comparing means for family factors and luck, is $9.75 + 24.85/2 = 17.3$ with $K(n_{jk} - 1) = 8$ df. Simple comparisons of the means revealed that, on the whole, family factors, then luck, were considered most important in contributing to poverty, whereas internal and external factors were least important. Each test was conducted at $\alpha_{pc} = .05/6 = .008$.

Tests on Interaction Effects. When interaction is found, main effects may not be as important. Interaction implies that simple contrasts between cell means of one variable will differ at some levels of the second variable. However, this may not be true of all such contrasts, in which case the main effect still is important.

The initial focus may be on simple main effects. Simple effects test for differences across one treatment at each level of the second variable—that is, a_1 versus a_2 versus a_3 versus a_4 at the level of b_1 (males) and again at the level of b_2 (females), as well as b_1 versus b_2 at each level of factor A. Because there are four levels of factor A and two levels of factor B, this yields a total of six simple-effects analyses. As is true of any simple-effects analysis, each SS is composed of main effects + interaction (i.e., ΣSS_A at $b_k = SS_A + SS_{A \times B}$). The error term depends on whether the SS refers to a group or repeated measures variable. With the repeated measures variable (A), *both* the main effect of A and of interaction are evaluated with $MS_{A \times swg}$ as the error term. Therefore the appropriate error term for simple main effects comparing the repeated measures means at each group level would be $MS_{A \times swg}$ or separate error terms for each group level—that is, each level is considered as a single-factor repeated measures study and error would be MS_{res}. Additionally, Looney and Stanley (1989) recommend that both univariate and multivariate analyses be conducted here as well, each at α/K. For these data α would equal .025.

The simple main-effects sum of squares for the group factor (B) consists of the group factor, whose error term is MS_{swg}, plus interaction SS, whose error term is $MS_{A \times swg}$. Therefore (Kirk, 1982), the appropriate error term for simple main effects of the group variable at each level of factor A is a pooling of the two terms:

$$MS_{pooled} = \frac{SS_{swg} + SS_{A \times swg}}{K(n_{jk} - 1) + (J - 1)[K(n_{jk} - 1)]}$$

As indicated in Winer (1971), the df associated with MS_{pooled} (within-cell variability) is less than $df_{swg} + df_{A \times swg}$ because it pools two heterogeneous variances. Moreover, the F ratio formed with MS_{pooled} as error does not have an F distribution. But the F can be approximated by altering df of MS_{pooled} according to a procedure proposed by Satterthwaite (in Winer, 1971):

$$df = \frac{(u + v)^2}{(u^2/f_1) + (v^2/f_2)}$$

where

u = SS_{swg},
v = $SS_{A \times swg}$,
f_1 = $K(n_j - 1)$, and
f_2 = $K(n_j - 1)(J - 1)$.

For the present data,

$$df = \frac{(67.2 + 211.6)^2}{(67.2^2/8) + (211.6^2/24)} = 31.986.$$

If df < 30 and variances are heterogeneous, separate error terms stem from pooling within-cell variances and reducing degrees of freedom to $K(n_{jk} - 1)$. For the data that were analyzed, pooled within-cell variances for simple main effects at, say, family factors, would be $(17.7 + 17.5)/2 = 17.6$, with df = 2(4) = 8 (see Table 5.1). A pooled error term, MS_{pooled}, would be $(67.2 + 211.6)/(8 + 24) = 8.712$. And to further protect against a type I error, each test should be performed at α/J. For the present data, $\alpha = .05/4 = .0125$.

Simple main effects that are significant and include more than two means can be further analyzed by simple contrasts between means. With regard to these post hoc analyses, special attention has to be given to the choice of the best test to use. Whereas the Bonferroni approach protects against the type I error for single-factor studies (Maxwell, 1980), this is not always true of two-factor mixed designs. These designs vary in degrees of departure from sphericity, group sizes, and homogeneity of covariance matrix, and data may be analyzed by weighted or unweighted means analyses. The Tukey, modified Tukey (separate error terms), Bonferroni, or multivariate procedures all led to inflated type I error rates following multiple simultaneous comparisons between means of groups that varied in the parameters, especially with unweighted means analyses. But a weighted mean analysis using the Bonferroni or a multivariate technique did limit the type I error rate. Moreover, the former was more powerful when three independent groups had 8 (vs. 4) repeated measures (Keselman & Keselman, 1988).

For the data that were analyzed, the interaction effect was significant (multivariate analysis). The group (gender) effect on each of the four attributions was assessed with separate, pooled within-cell variances of each test level with df equal to 1 and 8 and $\alpha_{pc} = .05/4 = .0125$. The attribution effect on males and on females each was evaluated at $\alpha_{pc} = .05/2 = .025$. Each F ratio used a separate residual error term and each first was evaluated with df = 1 and 4. The F ratios for both groups were significant at this level, and the ε adjustment was not required. They indicated that males and females attribute different causes to poverty. Simple main effects were followed by 12 simple comparisons, each tested at $\alpha = .05/12 = .004$ and df = 1 and 4. Only two differences emerged. Males attributed poverty more to luck than internal factors and females attributed poverty more to family factors than to luck.

Some have argued that the simple main-effect approach to analyzing interaction may not be justified, inasmuch as the SS based on simple effects of one factor is composed of the factor effect SS plus SS due to interaction (cf. Keppel, 1982; Kirk, 1982). Another argument is that H_0 for interaction is not consistent with H_0 for simple effects, here based on means (cf. Boik, 1979). These were the bases for introducing an alternate approach to understanding the nature of a significant interaction: partial interactions and interaction contrasts.

A *partial interaction* is a set of contrasts between two or more cell means corresponding to specific levels of one factor (e.g., a_1 vs. a_2) at each level of the second factor (e.g., at b_1 and b_2). With no interaction between the levels of, say, factor A and factor B, all contrasts will be the same and nonsignificant. If the contrasts differ at each level, then these levels interact with factor B. The general procedure is fully described by several authors (e.g., Boik, 1979; Keppel, 1982; Kirk, 1982) and essentially involves calculating an overall SS for each set of contrasts and determining their significance. However, although that procedure is appropriate for planned comparisons, it is not recommended for post hoc comparisons (cf. Boik, 1981). Instead, a procedure described by Boik and Kirk (1977) can be employed.

Here, the raw data are first transformed before the analysis, which consists of single df comparisons. Because the overall ratings of family factors exceeded those of all other factors, partial interactions were analyzed for family factors versus luck, versus internal causes, and versus external causes of poverty at the levels of males and females. Moreover, luck was attributed more importance than either internal or external causes, so this factor also was pitted against the latter two.

In all, two partial interactions were analyzed. Each of the two analyses (with 1 df) employed separate $MS_{A \times swg}$ as the error term. Of these, two F ratios were significant: ratings of family factors were higher than the remaining factors, but this factor did not interact with gender. However, the second partial interraction was significant, and, on the basis of the means, it could be concluded that males attributed more importance to luck (as a cause of poverty) than to internal and external factors, whereas females attributed less importance to luck. The fact that the partial interactions involving family causes of poverty were not significant shows that it is uniformally rated as most important by males and females.

An *interaction contrast* is the product of two contrasts, one of factor A and the other of factor B. It is determined by multiplying the contrasts of a set in, say, factor A by the coefficients of a set of contrasts in, say, factor B. Significance implies that the two variables interact for those levels. This more refined procedure is designed to more firmly pinpoint the source of the omnibus interaction and is used with more than two levels of each factor; with just two levels, all of the information needed to understand interaction is obtained by partial interactions (cf. Boik, 1979; Boik & Kirk, 1977; Kirk, 1982).

Quasi F Ratios

The designs discussed, on the whole, have assumed fixed-effect variables. Another common model includes at least one variable in which the levels are a random sample of all possible levels (i.e., a mixed-effect model). When this is the case, E(MS) components differ from those described and, in fact, may result in components for which no single error term is appropriate. (Derivations of E(MS) are discussed in detail in Keppel, 1982; Kirk, 1982; and Winer, 1971.) In this event it would be necessary to piece together MSs so that they form a ratio with one difference (the effect) between the numerator and denominator. Such F ratios are called quasi F ratios.

We have already examined the situation in which the group factor is considered a random effects variable. This changed the error term for testing the effect of the repeated measures variable, but otherwise produced no particular problem. Now we will consider an instance in which the group factor is manipulated and produces a fixed effect, but the repeated measures factor is a random sample of J levels. Say that an informal survey (for the data we analyzed) produced 25 different causes of poverty, and we randomly selected four of these. The E(MS)s are the following:

$$E(MS_B) = \sigma_\varepsilon^2 + \sigma_{\pi\alpha}^2 + J\sigma_\pi^2 + n_{jk}\,\sigma_{\alpha\beta}^2 + \left[nJ\sum\beta^2/(K-1)\right]$$

$$E(MS_{swg}) = \sigma_\varepsilon^2 + \sigma_{\pi\alpha}^2 + J\sigma_\pi^2$$

$$E(MS_A) = \sigma_\varepsilon^2 + \sigma_{\pi\alpha}^2 + nJ\sigma_\alpha^2$$

$$E(MS_{A \times B}) = \sigma_\varepsilon^2 + \sigma_{\pi\alpha}^2 + n_{jk}\,\sigma_{\alpha\beta}^2$$

$$E(MS_{A \times swg}) = \sigma_\varepsilon^2 + \sigma_{\pi\alpha}^2$$

In keeping with the usual criterion for the F ratio—that is, identical terms in numerator and denominator except for the addition of the treatment effect—there is no single error term for testing the group effect (factor B). The numerator E(MS$_B$) consists of

$$(A)\sigma_\varepsilon^2 + (B)\sigma_{\pi\alpha}^2 + (C)J\sigma_\pi^2 + (D)n_{jk}\sigma_{\alpha\beta}a^2 + \text{effect}.$$

The $E(MS_{swg}) = A + B + C$. This leaves $D + $ effect, two differences between the numerator and denominator. We need a denominator component that includes D, and it is present in $E(MS_{A\times B})$. If we add $E(MS_{A\times B})$ to $E(MS_{swg})$, we have

$$A + B + C + A + B + D = 2A + 2B + C + D.$$

This yields an extra A and B, the very terms of $E(MS_{A\times swg})$. Therefore, if $E(MS_{A\times swg})$ is subtracted from the above, the result is an appropriate error term:

$$\begin{aligned} E(MS_{swg}) + E(MS_{A\times B}) - E(MS_{A\times swg}) &= 2A + 2B + C + D \\ &= \sigma_\varepsilon^2 + \sigma_{\pi\alpha}^2 + J\sigma_\pi^2 + n_{jk}\sigma_{\alpha\beta}^2. \end{aligned}$$

The quasi F ratio thus becomes

$$F' = \frac{MS_B}{MS_{swg} + MS_{A\times B} - MS_{A\times swg}}.$$

The df for the denominator, according to Satterthwaite, are

$$df_{den} = \frac{(MS_{swg} + MS_{A\times B} - MS_{A\times swg})^2}{(MS_{swg}^2/df_{swg}) + (MS_{A\times B}^2/df_{A\times B}) + (MS_{A\times swg}^2/df_{A\times swg})}.$$

If we use the data of Table 5.1, then $F' = 1392.4/(8.4 + 52.067 - 8.817) = 26.958$ and denominator df $= (8.4 + 52.067 - 8.817)^2/[(8.4^2/8) + (52.067^2/3) + (8.817^2/24)] = 2.91$.

Because of the possibility of obtaining a negative error term when several are pieced together by adding and subtracting, another procedure is to add to the numerator MS rather than subtracting from the denominator to obtain an appropriate F ratio. These quasi F ratios are on the order of $F' = (MS_1 + MS_2)/(MS_3 + MS_4)$, and their corresponding df are on the order of $(MS_1 + MS_2)^2/[(MS_1^2/df_1) + (MS_2^2/df_2)]$ for the numerator and a similar expression for the denominator with subscripts 3 and 4 in place of 1 and 2.

The robustness of the quasi F has been demonstrated for independent-groups designs and for a repeated measures situation involving one type of design: $S \times A(B)$. In this case subjects are repeatedly measured at all levels of A and B, but B (like S) is a random variable and its levels are nested within A, a fixed-effects variable (i.e., each level of A includes a different sample of B). Despite varying departures from sphericity, the quasi F was fairly robust in protecting against the type I error. This contrasts sharply with the usual F tests. Whether this robustness holds for other designs remains to be determined (Maxwell & Bray, 1986).

Pretest-Posttest Designs

A commonly used between-groups design employs one or more treatment/control groups that are pretested, exposed to treatment/control procedures, and posttested. There are two situations to which this type of design might apply. In the true experiment we can assume initial group equivalence on the dependent variable and other characteristics that might affect posttreatment measures. In the quasi-experiment, intact groups are tested and initial equivalency cannot be assumed. Because of this, statistical procedures ordinarily applied to pre- and posttreatment data have to be evaluated more cautiously. Adequate handling of such data from quasi-experimental groups designs has been dealt with extensively by Cook and Campbell (1979). The present discussion assumes group equivalence prior to treatment.

Among the hypotheses that can be tested with such data, the extent to which treatment differentially affects the various groups is of primary interest. In the absence of an "interaction" effect, a main effect of treatment is of interest. Several techniques have been used to analyze the data. These include (a) ignoring pretreatment scores and performing a one-way analysis on posttreatment scores (Cook & Campbell, 1979), (b) performing a split-plot analysis of variance for repeated measures (Brogan & Kutner, 1980; Grieve, 1981; Huck & McLean, 1975; Levin, 1981), (c) analyzing pre- and posttreatment difference or gain scores (Brogan & Kutner, 1980; Grieve, 1981; Huck & McLean, 1975; Levin, 1981), and (d) using pretest scores as covariates for analysis of covariance.

Although one-way analysis of variance is least preferred because pretest data are ignored, attention has focused on the remaining three tests. If the data are analyzed by repeated measures the usual assumptions of equal variance-covariance matrices among groups and sphericity of the pooled matrix apply (Grieve, 1981). However, Huck and

McLean (1975) noted that the parametric model actually is inappropriate for this type of situation; it includes the group-by-trials interaction ($\alpha\beta_{jk}$), which does not apply when pretest measures are taken *before* treatment is administered. As a result, what is calculated as a main effect for treatment actually reflects an effect only on posttreatment scores; an effect that is less than the E(MS) for treatment and leads to a conservative F test. Moreover, the interaction effect actually is another measure of the treatment effect (on posttreatment scores), but one that takes into account the pretest measure. As such, the same F ratio is obtained if this interaction effect is assessed or a one-way analysis of variance is performed on the gain scores (i.e., differences between pre- and posttreatment scores). Finally, if the pooled within-groups regression coefficient is approximately 1.00 (showing a close to perfect linear relationship between the pretest and posttest scores for all groups), then a one-way analysis of covariance (with pretest as the covariate) will yield the same MS for treatment and almost the same F ratio as does analysis of the gain scores—all of which reflects an effect of treatment, not interaction. On these bases, Huck and McLean maintain that a repeated measures analysis in this situation is no more revealing than a simple analysis of variance of gain scores. A main effect for trials is not of much interest; the same treatment effect will be revealed and post hoc comparisons would be made on gain scores. Others (e.g., Brogan & Kutner, 1980; Grieve, 1981; Levin, 1981) also have shown that the two procedures and their underlying assumptions are the same.

Analysis of covariance is an alternative approach to handling data of pretest-posttest designs, especially when the groups have been formed by random assignment. This, too, requires the same assumptiom as the gain score analysis—equal regresson slopes. (Analysis of variance performed on difference scores assumes that the pooled within-group regression coefficient is 1.00.) Thus the choice of tests reduces to gain score analysis or analysis of covariance (ANCOVA). If the pooled within-group regression coefficient is 1.00, both analyses will yield the same MS for treatment. But ANCOVA loses a degree of freedom for error, rendering the gain score analysis more powerful. However, if the regression coefficient is less than 1.00, the error term will be smaller in ANCOVA, resulting in a more powerful test.

Another analysis that has been suggested for this situation is performance of an analysis of covariance on the gain scores, with pretest scores as the covariate. The F test is the same as with the usual analysis of covariance, but adjusted means of the gain scores take into account the *amount of change* from pre- to posttreatment performance due to regression toward the mean. In contrast, adjusted means based on the usual analysis of covariance adjust the posttreatment means by taking into account that *portion of the mean* due to regression toward the mean (Laird, 1983).

Strength of Association
Between Independent and Response Variables

The extent to which total variability can be explained by the effects of the independent variables can be estimated by ω^2. In the perceived-importance-of-attributions example, all three effects were significant. Determination of degree of association is similar to the estimations for the other repeated measures situations except for the denominator. This becomes $SS_T + MS_{bs} + n_{jk}K(MS_{A \times swg})$. The MS_{bs} is MS between-subjects. For this study,

$$\omega^2 = \frac{SS_{A \times B} - (J - 1)(K - 1)MS_{A \times swg}}{SS_T + MS_{bs} + n_{jk}K(MS_{A \times swg})} = \frac{156.2 - (4 - 1)(2 - 1)8.817}{3163.6 + 162.178 + 5(2)8.817}$$

$$= 0.038$$

for interaction and indicates that approximately 3.80% of total variability in ratings is associated with the interaction between the effects of gender and particular attributions of poverty, a trivial amount. Moreover, ω^2 for the effect of attribution equals .3836 and indicates that about 38.36% of total variability in ratings is associated with attributed causes of poverty. Finally, ω^2 for the group effect is .4000 and indicates that approximately 40% of variability in ratings is associated with gender.

6. THREE-FACTOR STUDIES

Studies with Repeated Measures on One Factor

The accessibility of computers has made complex designs involving more than two factors increasingly popular. The logical extension of the split-plot or mixed design is a three-factor study with repeated measures on one factor. The group factors can be experimental or individual variables. You might vary palatability of reward (factor B) and its magnitude (factor C) and measure latency of a response over a series of trials (factor A). Individuals would be randomly assigned to the various BC combinations and then be repeatedly measured over the series of trials. You also might obtain samples of male and female preschool and kindergarten children who have been exposed to parental conflict (C) and are living at home or in a residence for battered women (B), and measure each child's perceived competence and social acceptance (A). Interest is in the childrens' perceptions as a function of residence and potential interaction effects of the three variables.

A similar, more elaborate study was conducted by Fantuzzo et al. (1991). Under the assumption that witnessing parental conflict (verbal and physical) will affect a youngster's feelings of competence and acceptance, and that living in a temporary shelter will have an additional impact, nonabused children from a Head Start program and from residences for battered women were administered a Pictorial Scale of Perceived Competence and Social Acceptance for Young Children. Each child compared herself or himself to pictures of children who were cognitively and physically low or high in competence and high or low in peer and maternal acceptance. Each child then received a rating on the four subscales of the test.

Partitioning of Sums of Squares. Here, too, the total deviation of scores from the grand mean is partitioned into a between-subjects and a within-subjects component. The between-subjects component again represents the difference between a subject's mean and the grand mean. Such a difference is due to membership in one of the two groups (factors B and C), the effect of the interaction between them (B × C), and the child's variability within the group (swg). Similarly, the within-subjects component represents the difference between a child's score and mean and is due to the level of the repeated measures factor that yielded the score (factor A), the interaction between that factor and one of the group memberships (A × B), the interaction between that factor and the second group membership (A × C), the interaction between that factor and joint group membership (A × B × C), and the particular effect of the repeated measures factor on that individual (A × swg).

In terms of the parametric model,

$$(Y_{ijkl} - \mu) = \beta_k + \gamma_l + \beta\gamma_{kl} + \pi_{i(kl)} + \alpha_j + \alpha\beta_{jk}$$
$$+ \alpha\gamma_{jl} + \alpha\beta\gamma_{jkl} + \alpha\pi_{ji(kl)} + \varepsilon_{ijkl},$$

where

β_k = fixed effect of one group membership, represented by $(\mu_{..k.} - \mu)$ and estimated by $(\overline{Y}_{..k.} - \overline{Y}_g)$ or simply $(\overline{Y}_k - \overline{Y}_g)$;

γ_l = fixed effect of the second group membership, represented by $(\mu_{...l} - \mu)$ and estimated by $(\overline{Y}_{...l} - \overline{Y}_g)$ or simply $(\overline{Y}_l - \overline{Y}_g)$;

$\beta\gamma_{kl}$ = interaction effect of joint groups membership, represented by $(\mu_{..kl} - \mu_{..k.} - \mu_{...l} + \mu)$ and estimated (in simpler form) by $(\overline{Y}_{kl} - \overline{Y}_k - \overline{Y}_l + \overline{Y}_g)$;

$\pi_{i(kl)}$ = effect of the subject, nested within factors B and C, represented by $(\mu_{i...} - \mu_{..kl})$ and estimated by $(\overline{Y}_i - \overline{Y}_{kl})$;

α_j = fixed effect of the repeated measures factor, represented by $(\mu_{.j..} - \mu)$ and estimated by $(\overline{Y}_j - \overline{Y}_g)$;

$\alpha\beta_{jk}$ = interaction effect of the repeated measures factor and one of the group memberships, represented by $(\mu_{.jk.} - \mu_{.j..} - \mu_{..k.} + \mu)$ and estimated by $(\overline{Y}_{jk} - \overline{Y}_j - \overline{Y}_k + \overline{Y}_g)$;

$\alpha\gamma_{jl}$ = interaction effect of the repeated measures factor and the second group membership, represented by $(\mu_{.j.l} - \mu_{.j..} - \mu_{...l} + \mu)$ and estimated by $(\overline{Y}_{jl} - \overline{Y}_j - \overline{Y}_l + \overline{Y}_g)$;

$\alpha\beta\gamma_{jkl}$ = interaction effects of the repeated measures factor and joint group membership, represented by $(\mu_{.jkl} + \mu_{.j..} + \mu_{..k.} + \mu_{...l} - \mu_{.jk.} - \mu_{.j.l} - \mu_{..kl} - \mu)$ and estimated by $(\overline{Y}_{jkl} + \overline{Y}_j + \overline{Y}_k + \overline{Y}_l - \overline{Y}_{jk} - \overline{Y}_{jl} - \overline{Y}_{kl} - \overline{Y}_g)$; and

$\alpha\pi_{ji(kl)}$ = effect of the repeated measures factor on the unique individual, represented by $(Y_{ijkl} - \mu_{.jkl} - \mu_{i...} + \mu_{..kl})$ and estimated by $(Y_{ijkl} - \overline{Y}_{jkl} - \overline{Y}_i + \overline{Y}_{kl})$.

If all estimations are squared, weighted by the appropriate number of scores contributing to each, and added together, the empirical model appropriate for this situation is

$$SS_T = SS_B + SS_C + SS_{B \times C} + SS_{swg} + SS_A + SS_{A \times B} + SS_{A \times C}$$
$$+ SS_{A \times B \times C} + SS_{A \times swg}.$$

The addition of one factor increases the number of main effects (by one) and interactions (by three). The same information is sought as in a two-factor design, but there is a difference. In the two-factor study,

TABLE 6.1
Perceived Competence and Acceptance[a]

	Males(c_1)				Females(c_2)			
	a_1	a_2	a_3	a_4	a_1	a_2	a_3	a_4
	MA	PA	CC	PC	MA	PA	CC	PC
Home (b_1)	6	6.5	9	10	5	6	7.3	10
	7	7.5	9	9.5	6	7	8	8.5
	8	9	11	12	6	7	8	11
	8	9.5	11	12	6	6.9	7	11
	11	12.5	15	16.5	7	8.1	9.7	14.5
$\overline{Y}_{jkl}$	8	9	11	12	6	7	8	11
Shelter (b_2)	4	4	5	5.5	4	4.5	5.8	5
	5	7	7	7	4	4.5	5.5	4
	5	6	7	7	4	5	7	6
	5	6	6	6.5	3	5	7	6
	6	7	10	9	5	6	9.7	9
$\overline{Y}_{jkl}$	5	6	7	7	4	5	7	6

NOTE: a. MA = maternal acceptance; PA = peer acceptance; CC = cognitive competence; PC = perceived competence.

a significant interaction may modify statements made about the effects of main factors. In the three-factor study, a significant triple (second-order) interaction modifies statements about first-order interaction effects.

Calculation of Sums of Squares. The example of a three-factor study with repeated measures on one factor involves male and female youngsters who have witnessed parental conflict (factor C) and are living at home or at a shelter (factor B), each of whom has been measured for cognitive and physical competence and peer and maternal acceptance (factor A). The intent is to determine whether perceived competence and acceptance differ as a function of the child's gender and/or of residence. The hypothetical data of Table 6.1 are measures based on responses to six pictures per subscale of the test. Here, MA = maternal acceptance, PA = peer acceptance, CC = cognitive competence, and PC = physical competence. The analysis is likely to be performed by computer. Each sum of squares is based on the squared estimation of a parameter, weighted by the number of scores contributing to each estimation.

TABLE 6.2
Summary Table for Three-Factor Study

Source	SS	df	MS	F
Between-Subjects	390.69	19		
Residence	195.31	1	195.31	20.866*
Gender	37.81	1	37.81	4.040
Residence × Gender	7.81	1	7.81	0.834
Within Group	149.76	16	9.36	
Within-Subjects	183.58	60		
Scale	128.44	3	42.81	82.805*
Scale × Residence	23.44	3	7.81	15.106*
Scale × Gender	0.94	3	0.31	0.600
Scale × Residence × Gender	5.94	3	1.98	3.830*
Scale × Within Group	24.82	48	0.517	

*$p < .05$.

Calculation of Mean Squares and F *Ratios.* Calculation of these sums of squares makes it clear that they are extensions of the two-factor mixed design. The summary table is identical, albeit longer, and the bases for the F ratios are the same; all appropriate for the fixed-effects model. The MS_{swg} is the error term for the between-subjects factors (B, C, and B × C). The $MS_{A×swg}$ is the appropriate error term for the within-subjects factor and interactions (A, A × B, A × C, and A × B × C).

As indicated in Table 6.2, overall perceived competence and acceptance was higher for youngsters living at home. Moreover, there were overall differences in measures of competence and acceptance. Most important, these measures varied as a joint function of the particular subscale and residence. The unadjusted F ratio for triple interaction also is significant. A determination of the precise effects and appropriate conclusions depends on whether the assumptions of the test have been met.

Assumptions Underlying This Mixed Model. The same assumptions apply to this, as to the two-factor, situation. Thus, because swg variances are pooled, all should be homogeneous. Likewise, the A × swg variances also are assumed to be homogeneous. In each case homogeneity may be tested by the ratio between the largest and smallest variance. The df of the former are JK and $(n - 1)$ df and of the latter are

JK and $(n - 1)(J - 1)$. Moreover, assumptions regarding homogeneous variance-covariance matrices for the four separate groups (males and females at home or in a shelter) and sphericity of the pooled matrices also apply to this situation.

Again, the tests for homogeneity of the matrices as well as sphericity are unduly sensitive to departures from normality, and the usual recommendation is to make the $\hat{\epsilon}$ or $\tilde{\epsilon}$ adjustment on degrees of freedom. For the present data, the dfs were reduced by a factor of $\hat{\epsilon} = .60005$ (for these data). The adjusted df are $.60005(3) = 1.8 = 2$ and $.60005(48) = 28.8 = 29$ and $F_{(.025)} \approx 4.22$. Accordingly, the triple interaction is not significant, whereas the effect of the subscales and the scale × residence interaction are significant.

Multivariate Approach. In line with the recommended procedure for exploratory mixed designs (Looney & Stanley, 1989), these data also were subjected to multivariate analyses, using orthgonal contrasts for each subject, with each effect tested at $\alpha = .025$. The results with tests by Pillai, Hotelling, and Wilk yielded conclusions identical to those of the univariate tests, save the triple interaction, which was significant. However, the variance-covariance matrices were all singular, and results can be distorted when the error matrix is singular or nearly so (Shine, 1984).

Analyses of Means. If the main effects are significant, these receive further attention. If more than two groups participated in the study, their means would be compared using MS_{swg} as error and adjusted degrees of freedom, if variances are homogeneous. If they are not, separate error terms consisting of pooled MS_{res} with consequent reduction in degrees of freedom should be used. And, as is true of the two-factor study, a within-groups main effect employs $MS_{A \times swg}$ as the error term, if circularity is tenable, or separate error terms if it is untenable. Kirk (1982) fully describes the method used to obtain the MSs. These analyses were conducted on the four subscale means. All six comparisons used $(K)(L)(n_{jk} - 1)(J - 1) = 48$ df, and each test was performed at $\alpha_{pc} = .05/6 = .008$. All differences were significant (unusual) and indicated that the children were most affected by parental conflict in terms of feeling less maternal acceptance and were least affected in terms of perception of their cognitive competence.

A significant, meaningful triple interaction is followed by analyses of two factors at each level of the third variable to detect the qualification in describing a first-order interaction. For example, you might determine whether there is an interaction between residence and subscale measures for males and for females. A significant first-order interaction is further analyzed as in a two-factor study (i.e., simple effects and single df contrasts) or analyses of partial interactions, followed by interaction contrasts for more than two levels of each variable. Each comparison requires adjustments in α_{pc} and the appropriate error term (usually separate) with a reduction in df, as described in Chapter 5.

In the event that focus is on a first-order interaction, the appropriate error term for a simple-effects analysis depends on the factors being compared. Those effects involving solely group factors (C at b_k or B at c_l) employ MS_{swg}. Those involving repeated measures (A at b_k, c_l, or bc_{kl}) use $MS_{A \times swg}$. Those involving a group factor at levels of A (B, C, BC at a_j) employ MS_{pooled}. A more conservative error term consists of pooling the separate MS_{swg} and $MS_{A \times swg}$ (only for those cells being compared) and evaluating F with denominator df consisting of $v(n_j - 1)$ with v = number of pooled variances (Kirk, 1982). In the present study, the focus is on the interaction between subscale measures of competence and acceptance and residence at home or in a shelter. In view of the results of the main-effect subscale means, it made sense to determine which of the subscale tests differed for the two residences. Each of the four contrasts employed MS_{pooled} with df adjusted according to the proposal by Satterthwaite. The results indicated only one significant difference: Children who resided in a shelter felt less physically competent than did children who lived at home.

Another alternate means analysis, with a quantitative independent variable, is trend analysis. A detailed example of such analyses is in Winer (1971). The orthogonal polynomial coefficients used to weight each score are based on the assumptions of equally spaced intervals and equal numbers of individuals per cell. Should an (unweighted) mean analysis be conducted with these coefficients, when the assumptions are violated (especially equal intervals), a trend might not be detected, whereas it would be if a weighted mean analysis were to be conducted (Hertzog & Rovine, 1985).

Studies with Repeated Measures on Two Factors

A three-factor study also may include two variables that are measured repeatedly and a third that is between-groups. A social issue that is troublesome today relates to teenage pregnancy and an adolescent's ability to care for her child. Many drop out of school, are un-employed, and live in poverty. These factors contribute to the poor quality of care the infant is likely to receive. The question is: How can we help the teenage mother become more nurturing? One possibility is a program that includes caregivers as models and that provides experience in interacting with a child, with feedback. Such a program was developed (Cooper, Dunst, & Vance, 1990). Our example is based on their study.

Assume that we enlist 10 teenagers who have had their first baby. Half are over 16 years old and half are younger. This is the between-groups factor (B). The program runs for 20 weeks, in a center for pre-school children, and includes on-the-job training, counseling, goal planning, and life-skill classes. Each teenager is paired with an expert caregiver, who simultaneously is a model for the new mother and pro-vides feedback when she interacts with a 1- to 2-year-old infant. Every 5 weeks, 20-minute segments of the interaction are videotaped (factor A). Finally, naive raters score each teenager for the extent to which she encourages the infant to interact with other people or toys (engaging behavior) and is responsive to the infant (factor C).

Partitioning of Sums of Squares. Consistent with previous analyses, the difference between any score and the grand mean is partitioned into a between-subjects and within-subjects component, each retaining their previous meanings. The between-subjects component consists of vari-ability due to the different groups (factor B) and differences within each group (swg). The within-subjects component consists of variability due to each repeated measures factor (A and C), interaction between the ef-fects of the group factor and each repeated measures factor (A × B and B × C), the effects of both repeated measures factors (A × C), and the ef-fects of all three factors (A × B × C). Finally, this component consists of the effect of the particular level of a repeated measures factor on a par-ticular individual (A × swg and C × swg), as well as the joint effect of particular levels of each repeated measures factor on the particular indi-vidual (A × C × swg).

These components assume interaction between individual and fac-tor effects; they are demonstrated in the following parametric model:

$$Y_{ijkl} - \mu = \beta_k + \pi_{i(k)} + \alpha_j + \alpha\beta_{jk} + \alpha\pi_{ji(k)} + \Gamma_l + \beta\Gamma_{kl} + \Gamma\pi_{li(k)} + \alpha\Gamma_{jl} + \alpha\beta\Gamma_{jkl} + \alpha\Gamma\pi_{jli(k)} + \varepsilon_{ijkl}$$

Only some of these parameters are new and require definition:

$\alpha\pi_{ji(k)}$ = effect of a particular level of repeated measures factor A on the particular individual nested within the group.

Γ_l = fixed effect of repeated measures factor C.

$\beta\Gamma_{kl}$ = effect of the interaction between repeated measures factor C and the group factor (B).

$\Gamma\pi_{li(k)}$ = effect of the particular level of repeated measures factor C on the particular individual.

$\alpha\Gamma_{jl}$ = effect of the interaction between the two repeated measures factors.

$\alpha\beta\Gamma_{jkl}$ = effect of the interaction between the three factors.

$\alpha\Gamma\pi_{jli(k)}$ = effect of a particular combination of levels of the repeated measures factors on the particular individual.

When all components are estimated and the deviations are squared and summed, the model for the analyses is

$$SS_T = SS_B + SS_{swg} + SS_A + SS_{A\times B} + SS_{A\times swg} + SS_C + SS_{B\times C} + SS_{C\times swg} + SS_{A\times C} + SS_{A\times B\times C} + SS_{AC\times swg}.$$

If the additive model applies, the components are reduced by $SS_{A\times swg}$, $SS_{C\times swg}$, and $SS_{A\times C\times swg}$ and in turn replaced by a pooled error term.

Computation of Sums of Squares. Hypothetical ratings of engaging (c_1) and responsive (c_2) behaviors are in Table 6.1. These data were re-analysed to demonstrate the increased power of this design. Here, each row now contains data from a single individual. Level b_1 represents the older group and b_2 the younger group. Moreover, summary tables are identical, as are main effects and interactions among the three variables. In fact, the only difference in analyses is the reduction in within-subjects error by the addition of two sums of squares: $SS_{C\times swg}$ and $SS_{AC\times swg}$.

The F Ratio. The formation of critical F ratios again depends on expected values of the main sources of variance to be evaluated. Essentially, these are extensions of E(MS) appropriate for the two-factor, completely randomized block design and the between-subjects factor, all assuming a fixed-effects statistical model. Thus, MS_{swg} is the error term for MS_B, $MS_{A\times swg}$ is the error term for MS_A and $MS_{A\times B}$, $MS_{C\times swg}$ is the error term for MS_C and $MS_{B\times C}$, and $MS_{AC\times swg}$ is the error term for $MS_{A\times C}$ and $MS_{A\times B\times C}$.

TABLE 6.3
Summary of Analysis of Variance

Source	SS	df	MS	F
Between-Subjects	326.90	9		
B(age)	195.31	1	195.31	11.87**
swg	131.59	8	16.45	
Within-Subjects	247.37	70		
A(time)	128.44	3	42.81	52.21**
A × B	23.44	3	7.81	9.52**
A × swg	19.70	24	0.82	
C(rating)	37.81	1	37.81	16.66**
B × C	7.81	1	7.81	3.44
C × swg	18.16	8	2.27	
A × C	0.94	3	0.31	1.48
A × B × C	5.94	3	1.98	9.43**
AC × swg	5.13	24	0.21	

$**p < .01.$

The final F ratios of the univariate analysis are summarized in Table 6.3. The results of the univariate and multivariate analyses are in complete agreement. They show that teenagers over 16 years old consistently scored higher than their younger counterparts, that scores increased as a function of time spent in the program, that ratings were higher for engaging behavior, and that the effects of time and age of the teenager interacted, as did all three variables. The increased sensitivity of this design, compared with the earlier study, is shown by the triple interaction, now clearly significant.

Assumptions Underlying the Analyses. Assumptions underlying these F tests are extensions of those underlying the completely randomized block design and between-groups two-factor design. The between-group variances ($MS_{swg}s$) are assumed to be homogeneous. Homogeneity of within-group variances is required to pool A × swg, C × swg and AC × swg. Each can be tested by F_{max} = largest MS/smallest MS. Additionally, a Bartlett test may be used to test homogeneity of the three subject-interaction variances. If they clearly are homogeneous, the additive model applies. The three components can be pooled to yield an error term with increased degrees of freedom.

The variance-covariance matrices for each cell involving interaction with a repeated measures factor (A × swg, C × swg, AC × swg) are assumed to be homogeneous and to have sphericity patterns. This is in accord with the analysis for the two-factor study and represents local sphericity. As delineated by Mendoza, Toothaker, and Crain (1976), local sphericity includes the matrices corresponding to the A and C combinations for each group of persons. For the present data there would be $a_1c_1, a_2c_1, \ldots a_4c_2$ for each of the two groups of teens. And, as with the completely randomized block design, local sphericity may exist when overall sphericity does not. If the matrices demonstrate sphericity, then the usual F test can be conducted with the usual df. If the overall matrix of combined levels of the repeated measures factors (i.e., a_1c_1, $a_2c_1, \ldots a_4c_2$) demonstrate sphericity—if there is no interaction between subject and factor variables—then a much more powerful test could be conducted. The error term is the pooled local error terms and df. Such a restrictive outcome is not likely; nor is it likely that the local matrices will exhibit circularity. Hence, because popular statistical programs routinely supply values for $\hat{\varepsilon}$ and $\tilde{\varepsilon}$, the df can be adjusted directly. For the present data the triple interaction was significant with unadjusted df and was evaluated first. The $\hat{\varepsilon}$ for the AC × swg matrix was .74349 and adjusted df for triple interaction are 3(.74349) = 2.23 = 2 and 24(.74349) = 17.8 = 18. The F ratio of 9.43 still is significant and modifies the first-order interaction.

Analyses of Mean Differences. If none of the interactions are significant, main effect means are compared. These use error terms appropriate to each factor. Differences among group means use MS_{swg} as error, those among factor A (repeated measures factor) employ $MS_{A \times swg}$, and those among factor C (repeated measures factor) use $MS_{C \times swg}$. If sphericity is violated, separate error terms for each comparison are appropriate. For our data, all six means comparisons between the four time intervals were conducted, with separate $MS_{A \times swg}$s, α_{pc} = .05/6 = .008, and df = 1 and 8. All comparisons, except that between the last two test times, were significant.

If only first-order interactions are significant (A × B, A × C, and/or B × C), appropriate analyses include simple effects, or partial interactions and interaction contrasts. The big problem is in selection of the appropriate error term. Because sphericity so seldom is demonstrated, the safest assumption is that it has been violated. In that case, if simple effects are analyzed, it is fruitful to consider the sources of variability that contribute to the comparison. As indicated earlier, the simple-effect sums of squares are composed of the main effect SS + interaction SS. Then,

$A \times B$ Interaction	Error SS
$\sum A$ at $b_k = SS_A + SS_{A \times B}$	$SS_{A \times swg}$
$\sum B$ at $a_j = SS_B + SS_{A \times B}$	$SS_{swg} + SS_{A \times swg}$
$A \times C$ Interaction	
$\sum A$ at $c_l = SS_A + SS_{A \times C}$	$SS_{A \times swg} + SS_{AC \times swg}$
$\sum C$ at $a_j = SS_C + SS_{A \times C}$	$SS_{C \times swg} + SS_{AC \times swg}$
$B \times C$ Interaction	
$\sum B$ at $c_l = SS_B + SS_{B \times C}$	$SS_{swg} + SS_{C \times swg}$
$\sum C$ at $b_k = SS_C + SS_{B \times C}$	$SS_{C \times swg}$

As recommended, separate error terms with reduced df will yield a more conservative test but provide greater protection against a type I error. For example, a test of factor A at b_1 (older teenagers) requires $SS_{A \times swg}$ for that group of individuals and degrees of freedom reduced to $(4 - 1)(5 - 1) = 12$ for the error component. Post hoc comparisons would be conducted as described earlier.

If the triple interaction is significant, this component receives attention. In our example, the triple interaction was significant, as was that between time of the test (A) and age of the teenager (B), which may depend on which behavior was being rated: engaging or responsiveness. Therefore, separate analyses are required for each level of factor C. Two sets of partial interactions were done, one for each behavior, according to the method recommended by Boik and Kirk (1977). Ratings of the first two and of the last two time intervals were transformed to form two new variables. The F ratio for responsiveness was not significant, whereas that for engaging behavior was ($p < .05$), showing that older teens improved their ratings by the last two test periods.

Missing Data

All analyses were performed under the assumption that each subject was measured the same number of times. This is more the exception than the rule. Equipment may break down; persons may become ill, forget to appear for a session, or refuse to participate any longer. Assuming that data are missing on a random basis, unrelated to a particular treatment and/or personality characteristic that would render the sample nonrepresentative, a variety of techniques are available for analyzing such data. You may discard the data and replace the subject. Indeed, the default option of most statistical programs is to ignore cases with missing data. In this case, especially for factorial studies, you may perform an analysis of variance for unweighted means (Winer, 1971: pp. 599-603). Several techniques are available to "fill in" missing values when the program involves regression analysis (Cohen & Cohen, 1983: pp. 275-299) or some attempt to estimate the missing values by an iterative process. All missing values, save one, are "guessestimated." The one is estimated by values of surrounding scores. The replacement value is entered and the process repeated for remaining missing values (Kirk, 1982: pp. 268-270). Along with this a df is lost from SS_{res} and SS_T for each missing value.

An Actual Study

The study by Fantuzzo et al. (1991) incorporates much of what has been described. Basically, 84 youngsters and their mothers from Head Start Centers and 23 similar pairs from shelters for battered wives (all low income) participated. In an effort to learn the extent to which children living at home or in a temporary shelter are affected by exposure to parental abuse, each mother was paid to complete two questionnaires: one measured abuse (at home: none, verbal, or verbal and physical; at a shelter: verbal and physical) and the other measured her child's adjustment. Each child was administered the pictorial scale measuring the child's perception of competence and acceptance. Results were analyzed by group membership (abuse), gender, and scale ratings.

The adjustment main effect (corrected df) was significant, as was interaction between adjustment and abuse type. More than 40% of adjustment variability was associated with abuse type. Tukey tests showed that adjustment problems were associated with viewing both types of abuse by children living in the shelter and at home.

Analysis of the child's perceptions also revealed a scale main effect and an interaction between scale responses and abuse type.

Omega squared revealed that 5% of variability in competency and acceptance was associated with abuse type. Post hoc analyses used the Tukey test and revealed that children living in a temporary shelter who witnessed both types of maternal abuse perceived themselves to experience the least amount of maternal acceptance.

REFERENCES

BARCIKOWSKI, R. S., and ROBEY, R. R. (1983) "Decisions in single group repeated measures analysis: Statistical tests and three computer packages." American Statistician 38: 148-150.

BOIK, R. J. (1979) "Interactions, partial interaction, and interaction contrasts in the analysis of variance." Psychological Bulletin 86(5): 1084-1089.

BOIK, R. J. (1981) "A priori tests in repeated measures designs: Effects of nonsphericity." Psychometrika 46(3): 241-255.

BOIK, R. J., and KIRK, R. E. (1977) "A general method for partitioning sums of squares of treatments and interactions in the analysis of variance." Educational and Psychological Measurement 37: 1-9.

BOX, G. E. P. (1954) "Some theorems on quadratic forms applied in the study of analysis of variance problems: II. Effects of inequality of variance and of correlation between errors in the two-way classification." Annals of Mathematical Statistics 25: 484-498.

BRAY, J. H., and MAXWELL, S. E. (1985) Multivariate Analysis of Variance. Beverly Hills, CA: Sage.

BROGAN, D. R., and KUTNER, M. H. (1980) "Comparative analysis of pretest-posttest research designs." American Statistician 34(4): 229-232.

BROWN, M. B., and FORSYTHE, A. B. (1974) "The small sample behavior of some statistics which test the equality of several means." Technometrics 16(1): 129-132.

COHEN, J., and COHEN, P. (1983) Applied Multiple Regression/Correlation Analysis for the Behavioral Sciences (2nd ed.). Hillsdale, NJ: Lawrence Erlbaum.

COHEN, M., and RIEL, M. (1989) "The effect of distant audiences on students' writing." American Educational Research Journal 26(2): 143-159.

COLE, D. A., VANDERCOOK, T., and RYNDERS, J. (1988) "Comparison of two peer interaction programs: Children with and without severe disabilities." American Educational Research Journal 25(3): 415-439.

COLLIER, R. O., BAKER, F. B., MANDEVILLE, G. K., and HAYES, T. F. (1967) "Estimates of test size for several test procedures based on conventional variance ratios in the repeated measures design." Psychometrika 32(2): 339-352.

COOK, D. T., and CAMPBELL, D. T. (1979) Quasi-Experimentation: Design & Analysis Issues for Field Settings. Chicago: Rand McNally.

COOPER, C. S., DUNST, C. J., and VANCE, S. D. (1990) "The effect of social support on adolescent mothers' styles of parent-child interaction as measured on three separate occasions." Adolescence 25(97): 49-57.

DODD, D. G., and SCHULTZ, R. F., Jr. (1973) "Computational procedures for estimating magnitude of effect for some analysis of variance designs." Psychological Bulletin 79(6): 391-395.

EDWARDS, A. L. (1985) Experimental Design in Psychological Research (5th ed.). New York: Harper & Row.

74

FANTUZZO, J. W., DePAOLA, L. M., LAMBERT, L., MARTINO, T., ANDERSON, G., and SUTTON, S. (1991) "Effects of interparental violence on the psychological adjustment and competencies of young children." Journal of Counseling and Clinical Psychology 59(2): 258-265.

GEISSER, S., and GREENHOUSE, S. W. (1958) "An extension of Box's results on the use of the F distribution in multivariate analysis." Annals of Mathematical Statistics 29: 885-891.

GREENHOUSE, S. W., and GEISSER, S. (1959) "On methods in the analysis of profile data." Psychometrika 24(2): 95-112.

GRIEVE, A. P. (1981) "Letter to the editor." American Statistician 35(3): 177-178.

GRIEVE, A. P. (1984) "Tests of sphericity of normal distributions and the analysis of repeated measures designs." Psychometrika 49(2): 257-267.

HARRIS, G. T., RICE, M. E., and PRESTON, D. L. (1989) "Staff and patient perceptions of the least restrictive alternatives for the short-term control of disturbed behavior." Journal of Psychiatry & Law 13: 239-262.

HAYES, W. L. (1988) Statistics (4th ed.). New York: Holt, Rinehart & Winston.

HERTZOG, C., and ROVINE, M. (1985) "Repeated-measures analysis of variance in developmental research: Selected issues." Child Development 56: 787-809.

HIRST, M. K. (1988) "Intrinsic motivation as influenced by task interdependence and goal setting." Journal of Applied Psychology 73(1): 96-101.

HOLLAND, B. S., and COPENHAVER, M. D. (1988) "Improved Bonferroni-type multiple testing procedures." Psychological Bulletin 104(1): 145-149.

HUCK, S. W., and McLEAN, R. A. (1975) "Using a repeated measures ANOVA to analyze the data from a pretest-posttest design: A potentially confusing task." Psychological Bulletin 82(4): 511-518.

HUYNH, H. (1978) "Some approximate tests for repeated measurement designs." Psychometrika 43(2): 161-175.

HUYNH, H., and FELDT, L. S. (1970) "Conditions under which mean square ratios in repeated measurements designs have exact F-distributions." Journal of the American Statistical Association 65: 1582-1589.

HUYNH, H., and FELDT, L. S. (1976) "Estimation of the Box correction for degrees of freedom from sample data in randomized block and split-plot designs." Journal of Educational Statistics 1(1): 69-82.

HUYNH, H., and FELDT, L. S. (1980) "Performance of traditional F tests in repeated measures designs under covariance heterogeneity." Communications in Statistics—Theory and Methods A9(1): 61-74.

HUYNH, H., and MANDEVILLE, G. K. (1979) "Validity conditions in repeated measures designs." Psychological Bulletin 86: 964-973.

IMHOF, J. P. (1962) "Testing the hypothesis of no fixed main-effects in Scheffé's mixed model." Annals of Mathematical Statistics 33: 1085-1095.

IVERSEN, G. R., and NORPOTH, H. (1976) Analysis of Variance (2nd ed). Beverly Hills, CA: Sage.

JACCARD, J., and ACKERMAN, L. (1985) "Repeated measures analysis of means in clinical research." Journal of Consulting and Clinical Psychology 53(3): 426-428.

KEPPEL, G. (1982) Design & Analysis: A Researcher's Handbook (2nd ed.). Englewood Cliffs, NJ: Prentice-Hall.

KESELMAN, H. J. (1982) "Multiple comparisons for repeated measures means." Multivariate Behavioral Research 17: 87-92.

KESELMAN, H. J., and KESELMAN, J. C. (1987) "Type I error control and the power to detect factorial effects." British Journal of Mathematical and Statistical Psychology 40: 196-208.

KESELMAN, H. J., and KESELMAN, J. C. (1988) "Repeated measures multiple comparison procedures: Effects of violating multisample sphericity in unbalanced designs." Journal of Educational Statistics 13(3): 215-226.

KESELMAN, H. J., MENDOZA, J. L., ROGAN, J. C., and BREEN, L. J. (1980) "Testing the validity conditions of repeated measures F tests." Psychological Bulletin 87: 479-481.

KESELMAN, H. J., ROGAN, J. C., and GAMES, P. A. (1981) "Robust tests of repeated measures means in educational and psychological research." Educational and Psychological Measurement 41: 163-173.

KIRK, R. E. (1982) Experimental Design: Procedures for the Behavioral Sciences (2nd ed.). Belmont, CA: Brooks/Cole.

LAIRD, N. (1983) "Further comparative analyses of pretest-posttest research designs." American Statistician 37(4): 329-330.

LEVIN, J. R. (1981) "Letter to the editor." American Statistician 35(3): 178-179.

LOONEY, S. W., and STANLEY, W. B. (1989) "Exploratory repeated measures analysis for two or more groups." American Statistician 43(4): 220-225.

MAXWELL, S. E. (1980) "Pairwise multiple comparisons in repeated measures designs." Journal of Educational Statistics 5(3): 269-287.

MAXWELL, S. E., and ARVEY, R. D. (1982) "Small sample profile analysis with many variables." Psychological Bulletin 92(3): 778-785.

MAXWELL, S. E., and BRAY, J. H. (1986) "Robustness of the quasi F statistic to violations of sphericity." Psychological Bulletin 99(3): 416-421.

McCALL, R. B., and APPLEBAUM, M. I. (1973) "Bias in the analysis of repeated-measures designs: Some alternative approaches." Child Development 44: 401-415.

MENDOZA, J. L., TOOTHAKER, L. E., and CRAIN, B. R. (1976) "Necessary and sufficient conditions for F ratios in the L × J × K factorial design with two repeated factors." Journal of the American Statistical Association 71(356): 992-993.

MITZEL, H. C., and GAMES, P. A. (1981) "Circularity and multiple comparisons in repeated measures designs." British Journal of Mathematical and Statistical Psychology 34: 253-259.

MOORE, J. W., JENSEN, B., and HAUCK, W. E. (1990) "Decision-making processes of youth." Adolescence 25(99): 583-592.

NAMBOODIRI, K. (1984) Matrix Algebra. Beverly Hills, CA: Sage.

O'BRIEN, R. G., and KAISER, M. K. (1985) "MANOVA method for analyzing repeated measures designs: An extensive primer." Psychological Bulletin 97(2): 316-333.

O'CONNELL, J. M. (1988) "Several effects of behavioral cost on pigeon's reactivity to food and to Pavlovian signals for food." Journal of Experimental Psychology: Animal Behavior Processes 14(4): 339-348.

OLSON, C. L. (1976) "On choosing a test statistic in multivariate analysis of variance." Psychological Bulletin 83(4): 579-586.

PILLAI, K. C. S. (1955) "Some new test criteria in multivariate analysis." Annals of Mathematical Statistics 26: 117-121.

PUSEN, C., ERICKSON, J. R., HUE, C. W., and VYAS, A. P. (1988) "Priming from category members on retrieval of other category members: Positive and negative effects." Journal of Experimental Psychology: Learning, Memory, and Cognition 14(4): 627-640.

ROGAN, J. C., KESELMAN, H. J., and MENDOZA, J. L. (1979) "Analysis of repeated measurements." British Journal of Mathematical and Statistical Psychology 32: 269-286.

ROMANIUK, J. G., LEVIN, J. R., and HUBERT, L. J. (1977) "Hypothesis-testing procedures in repeated-measures designs: On the road map not taken." Child Development 48: 1757-1760.

ROUANET, H., and LÉPINE, D. (1970) "Comparison between treatments in a repeated-measurement design: ANOVA and multivariate methods." British Journal of Mathematical and Statistical Psychology 23(2): 147-163.

SHINE, L. C., II. (1984) "Using multivariate techniques to analyze within-subject effects in univariate ANOVA repeated measures designs." Educational and Psychological Measurement 44: 85-94.

STACEY, B. G., SINGER, M. S., and RITCHIE, G. (1989) "The perception of poverty and wealth among teenage university students." Adolescence 24(93): 193-206.

STEVENS, J. (1986) Applied Multivariate Statistics for the Social Sciences. Hillsdale, NJ: Lawrence Erlbaum.

WINER, B. J. (1971) Statistical Principles in Experimental Design (2nd ed.). New York: McGraw-Hill.

WOODWARD, J., CARNINE, D., and GERSTEN, R. (1988) "Teaching problem solving through computer simulations." American Educational Research Journal 25(1): 72-86.

ABOUT THE AUTHOR

ELLEN R. GIRDEN is Professor of Psychology at the School of Psychology of Nova University. She received her B.A. and M.A. from Brooklyn College and her Ph.D. from Northwestern University. She has several articles published in the areas of physiological psychology and general experimental psychology, and she has supervised more than 20 doctoral dissertation research projects. Her current research interests are in the management of stress by individuals with diabetes, and her primary teaching focus is on analysis of variance and research methodology.

Quantitative Applications in the Social Sciences

(a Sage University Papers Series)

$8.95 each

Place
Stamp
here

SAGE PUBLICATIONS, INC.
P.O. BOX 5084
NEWBURY PARK, CALIFORNIA 91359—9924